Clic!

Livre de l'étudiant

Renewed Framework

Danièle Bourdais
Sue Finnie
Lol Briggs
Michael Spencer

3 *Star*

OXFORD
UNIVERSITY PRESS

Oxford University Press

Great Clarendon Street, Oxford OX2 6DP

Oxford University Press is a department of the University of Oxford. It furthers the University's objective of excellence in research, scholarship, and education by publishing worldwide in

Oxford New York

Auckland Cape Town Dar es Salaam Hong Kong Karachi Kuala Lumpur Madrid Melbourne Mexico City Nairobi New Delhi Shanghai Taipei Toronto

With offices in

Argentina Austria Brazil Chile Czech Republic France Greece Guatemala Hungary Italy Japan Poland Portugal Singapore South Korea Switzerland Thailand Turkey Ukraine Vietnam

Oxford is a registered trade mark of Oxford University Press in the UK and in certain other countries

British Library Cataloguing in Publication Data

Data available

ISBN-13: 978 0 19 912788 7

10 9 8 7 6 5 4 3 2 1

Printed in Singapore by KHL Printing Co Pte Ltd

Paper used in the production of this book is a natural, recyclable product made from wood grown in sustainable forests. The manufacturing process conforms to the environmental regulations of the country of origin.

Acknowledgements
The authors and publisher would like to thank the following people for their help and advice:
Julie Green; Anna Lise Gordon; Sarah Provan; Rachel Sauvain; Marie-Thérèse Bougard; Teresa Adams; Sarah MacDonald; Tim Crapper, Aylesbury Grammar School, Aylesbury; Jan Harwood, Kingsdown School, Swindon; Julie Thomas, Marlwood School, Alveston; Crista Hazell, John Cabot City Technology College, Bristol; Emma Charrot, Burford School, Burford; Pierre Traore, St Gregory the Great RC Secondary School, Oxford; Terry Smith, Cooper School, Bicester; Rachel Gill, Stamford High School, Ashton Under Lyne; Stella Pearson, Our Lady's RC High School, Royton; Jane Bailey, Wellacre Technology College, Manchester; Elaine Kay, Altrincham College of Arts, Altrincham; John McStocker, Oulder Hill Community School, Rochdale; Sarah Allen, George Tomlinson School, Bolton; Sarah Ward, Flixton Girls' High School, Manchester; Joanne Roberts, Plant Hill Arts College, Manchester; Helen Dougan, The Hollins Technology College, Accrington; Air-Edel Associates Ltd

Video contributors: Florian Galera, Cyrielle Portiguatti, Franck Martinez, Marie Torresani, Isis Nesta, Charlie Gouin, Anthony Leydet

The publishers would like to thank the following for permission to reproduce photographs:
8t Stock Connection Distribution/Alamy; **10**tr Charles Gullung/Zefa/Corbis UK Ltd; **19** Daniel Day/Iconica/Getty Images; **20** iStockphotos; **25**t Directphoto/Alamy; **25**b Jochen Tack/Alamy; **28**tl Rault Jean Francois Kipa/Corbis UK Ltd; **28**cl Bertrand Guay/AFP/Getty Images; **28**bl Olivier Laban-Mattei/AFP/Getty Images; **28**tr c.Miramax/Everett/Rex Features; **28**cr c.20thC.Fox/Everett/Rex Features; **28**br Sipa Press/Rex Features; **28**c 'LOFT STORY' – THE FRENCH VERSION OF BIG BROTHER – 02 MAY; 201/Rex Features; **28**tcl Valery Hache/AFP/Getty Images; **28**tcr Sipa Press/Rex Features; **29** Martyn F. Chillmaid; **30**tl DREAMWORKS/ ALBUM/akg-images; **30**cl Ronald Grant Archive; **30**bl Everett Collection/Rex Features; **30**tr Ronald Grant Archive; **30**cr Ronald Grant Archive; **30**br c.Universal/Everett/Rex Features; **30**c Everett Collection/Rex Features; **31** Ronald Grant Archive; **32**c Pierre Minier – Ouest Medias/e/Corbis UK Ltd; **32**b Uli Wiesmeier/Zefa/Corbis UK Ltd; **32**a Christian Liewig/Liewig Media /Corbis UK Ltd; **32**d www.24rollers.com; **32**e Andres Kudacki/Corbis UK Ltd; **39** www.24rollers.com; **44**t c.Universal/Everett/Rex Features; **44**b Arnaud Chicurel/hemis.fr/Getty Images; **45**b 318; Gallo Images/Corbis UK Ltd; **46**c EUROLINES MEDIA OFFICE; **46**b Brittany Ferries; **46**l STUDIO CANAL/ UNIVERSAL FOCUS/ W/akg-images; **46**2 c.Universal/Everett/Rex Features; **46**3 c.Universal/Everett/Rex Features; **46**4 c.Universal/Everett/Rex Features; **46**5 c.Universal/Everett/Rex Features; **46**a Philippe Delafosse/Air France Corporate; **46**d Martyn F. Chillmaid; **46**e Chad Ehlers/Stone/Getty Images; **46**f Peter Bowater/Alamy; **46**g Peugeot Motor Company Ltd; **46**h Tetra Images/Alamy; **47** vario images GmbH & Co.KG/Alamy; **50**c Arnaud Chicurel/hemis.fr/Getty Images; **50**b Art On File/Corbis UK Ltd; **59**t 318; Gallo Images/Corbis UK Ltd; **59**b World Wildlife Fund for Nature; **62**b Steve Niedorf Photography/Getty Images; **64**d Martyn F. Chillmaid; **64**e Martyn F. Chillmaid; **64**f Martyn F. Chillmaid; **64**i Martyn F. Chillmaid; **68**1 Tina Lorien/iStockphoto; **68**2 J.riou/Photocuisine/Corbis UK Ltd; **68**3 Photographers Direct/Steve Hill Photography; **68**4 Nicholas Pitt/Alamy; **77** Horacio Villalobos/Epa/Corbis UK Ltd; **80**tl Patrick Robert/Sygma/Corbis UK Ltd; **80**tc H. Armstrong Roberts/Retrofile/Getty Images; **80/81**t Nokia; **81**b PhotoAlto/Alamy; **83** Patrick Robert/Sygma/Corbis UK Ltd; **84**1 Nokia; **84**2 JUPITERIMAGES/ ABLESTOCK/Alamy; **84**3 Apple Computer Inc; **84**4 Chris King/Oxford University Press; **84**5 Zooid Pictures; **84**6 Fujifilm UK Limited; **84**7 Tony Cordoza/Alamy; **84**8 Goodmans/Alba plc; **95**l Photodisc/Alamy; **95**r PhotoAlto/Alamy; **98**t John Walmsley/educationphotos.co.uk; **98**b Oxford University Press; **99**b Frank Trapper/Corbis UK Ltd; **101**t John Walmsley/educationphotos.co.uk; **101**b Jean-Philippe Ksiazek/AFP/Getty Images; **102**1 i love images/Alamy; **102**2 Picture Contact/Alamy; **102**3 Glyn Thomas/Alamy; **102**4 Comstock Select/Corbis UK Ltd; **102**5 UpperCut Images/Alamy; **102**6 Kelly Redinger/Design Pics/Corbis UK Ltd; **102**7 Janine Wiedel Photolibrary/Alamy; **102**8 Image100/Corbis UK Ltd; **102**9 Mm Productions/Corbis UK Ltd; **104**1 JUPITERIMAGES/ Comstock Images/Alamy; **104**2 Oxford University Press; **104**4 Martyn F. Chillmaid; **104**5 Steve Skjold/Alamy; **104**6 Martyn F. Chillmaid; **104**7 Helene Rogers/Alamy; **105**l c.Universal/Everett/Rex Features; **105**r Frank Trapper/Corbis UK Ltd; **111** Lucie Bertaud; **113** Richard Broadwell/Alamy; **121** Gideon Mendel/Corbis UK Ltd.

All other photographs supplied by Jules Selmes and Oxford University Press.

Illustrations by:
Kessia Beverley Smith, James Elston, Bill Greenhead, John Hallett, Gemma Hastilow, Abel Ippolito, Nigel Paige, Andy Parker, Tom Percival, Olivier Prime, Pulsar, Pete Smith, Theresa Tibbets, Enzo Troiano

All other artwork: Oxford University Press

Bienvenue à  Clic! 3

Welcome to *Clic! 3* where you will

- further your learning and understanding of French
- find out interesting facts about France, French-speaking countries and the people who live and work there
- find out why learning a language is important for you

Here are the characters you will meet on the *Clic! vidéo*. You'll find out what jobs they do, why they like them and what their ambitions are.

Florian

Charlie

Marie

Isis

Anthony

Franck

Cyrielle

Symbols and headings you will find in the book: what do they mean?
Look through the book and find an example of each one.

Watch the video

Be careful!

TEST A quick revision test to check what you have learnt

A listening activity

A speaking activity

(B → A) Now swap roles with your partner (in a speaking activity)

A video activity

A reading activity

A writing activity

 **Grammaire** A grammar activity

 Stratégies A learning skills activity

 Défi! A challenge

 Important words or phrases

Labo-langue	Grammar explanations and practice, learning strategies and pronunciation practice
Blog-notes	Activities linked to video blog (in preparation for the checklist in the *En solo* Workbook)
clic.fr	Information about France
Vocabulaire	Unit vocabulary list
On chante!	A song
Lecture	Reading pages
En plus	Reinforcement and extension activities
Grammaire	Grammar reference
Glossaire	Bilingual glossary

Table des matières

Unit	Page	Contexts	Language/Grammar	Learning strategies
Départ	6	Introduction to the characters who feature on the *Clic! vidéo*, what their jobs might be and why languages are important to them		
1 Premiers contacts	8	Meeting and greeting new people; asking someone out; accepting/declining invitations; arranging time and place to meet; keeping in touch with friends	*Tu veux aller avec moi...? Tu viens avec moi...? On va...? On se retrouve...? Non, désolé(e), je ne peux pas. Je veux bien. J'envoie des SMS. Je voudrais...* devoir/pouvoir/vouloir *+ infinitive*	Learning new words
C'est la vie	16	Florian: youth leader at an after school club and summer camp	Depuis *+ present tense*	
Labo-langue	18		Present tense verbs: regular and irregular	
2 À mon avis	26	Discussing TV programmes and films and giving opinions; talking about sports	Different TV programmes *(un feuilleton/un jeu télévisé)* and film genres *(un film de guerre/une comédie);J'ai aimé... Je n'ai pas aimé... C'est un film à éviter. C'était ennuyeux.* sport; *c'était/j'étais/tu étais*	Listening skills: listening for gist, intonation, emphasis
C'est la vie	34	Charlie: basketball player	Perfect tense	
Labo-langue	36		Perfect tense with *avoir/être*	
3 V comme voyages	44	Choosing how to travel and where to stay; visiting Paris	Choosing means of transport; preferences; comparatives *(Je préfère prendre le bus./Le train est plus écolo;* types of accommodation; superlatives *(le, la, les + plus/le, la, les + moins);* planning a visit; aller *+ infinitive*	Reading longer texts: reading for gist, identifying key words
C'est la vie	52	Cyrielle: trainee in a tourist office	Question forms; superlatives	
Labo-langue	54		Verb + infinitive *(aller/il faut/aimer/pouvoir/vouloir/pour + infinitive)*	

Unit	Page	Contexts	Language/Grammar	Learning strategies
4 Savoir-vivre	62	Staying with a French family; meal times in France; helping around the house; discussing differences between life in France and Great Britain	Different food items (un yaourt/les chips); being polite at the table (Vous pouvez me passer la pizza?); using negatives (ne...pas/plus/jamais/rien); household tasks (ranger la chambre/faire la vaisselle/passer l'aspirateur); pouvoir; adverbs of time/frequency (tous les jours/souvent)	Coping with unknown vocabulary
C'est la vie	70	Marie and Isis: two teenagers who have lived with a foreign family	Perfect tense	
Labo-langue	72		Negative expressions; using different tenses in longer sentences	
5 Découvrir le monde	80	Discussing what you are and are not allowed to do; comparing gadgets now and in the 1950s; discussing ways to be more environmentally friendly	Discussing what you have the right to do (Je peux/Je ne peux pas m'habiller comme je veux/me coucher quand je veux/avoir un job.); emphatic pronouns (moi/toi/lui/elle); gadgets now and from the 1950s (un portable/un lecteur DVD/un baladeur MP3/un tourne-disque/des jeux de société); discussing ways to be environmentally friendly (Respectez la nature./Économisez l'eau.)	Writing strategies
C'est la vie	88	Anthony: a young man who raises awareness about protecting the environment	Il faut/Il ne faut pas + infinitive	
Labo-langue	90		Talking about the past; imperfect tense	
6 Préparer l'avenir	98	Discussing the future: choosing subjects; what jobs you'd like to do; part-time jobs and ambitions	Saying what subjects you'll choose and why (L'année prochaine, je vais faire sciences, maths, français.../C'est ma matière préférée./Je suis fort(e)/nul(le)./Ça m'intéresse; different jobs (chanteuse/pilote de ligne); recognising the future tense; part-time jobs (Je travaille dans un magasin./Je vends des glaces.)	Writing: perfecting your written work
C'est la vie	106	Franck: supervisor at a school	Future plans; qualities needed to do the job	
Labo-langue			Talking about the future: the present tense; aller + infinitive; je voudrais + infinitive; future tense; using different tenses	

Départ
Bienvenue à Clic! 3

Clic! *vidéo takes you to the south of France. You'll meet six young French people who live in and around Marseille. They'll tell you about the jobs they do.*

Florian

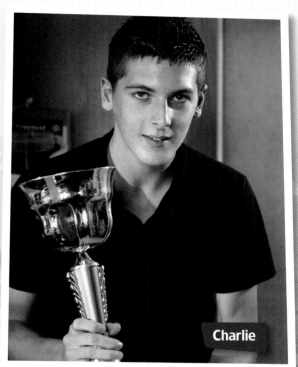

Charlie

Cyrielle

Anthony

Marie

Franck

READING
1a Lis et regarde les photos. À ton avis, c'est qui?

a Elle travaille à l'office du tourisme de Marseille.

b Il travaille dans une association de protection de l'environnement.

c Il est surveillant dans un collège. Il s'occupe des élèves quand ils n'ont pas cours.

d Il a 16 ans. Il joue au basket en ligue de championnat de France.

e Il est moniteur dans une colonie de vacances. Il adore les enfants.

f Elle habite à Marseille. L'année dernière, elle a travaillé en Grande-Bretagne, dans une famille.

1b Écoute et vérifie.

SPEAKING
2 À ton avis, une langue étrangère, c'est utile pour qui? Discutez en anglais en groupes.

Défi!

Do some research on the Internet or at the library and find out five facts about the city of Marseille. Compare your information with a partner.

Who would you like to do a work placement with? Why? When you've met all six people, answer the question again! Is your answer the same?

Pourquoi apprendre le français?

Pour se faire des amis francophones et garder contact

Premier jour de vacances: présente-toi!

Voir pages 10–11.

Comment inviter une fille/un garçon?

Voir pages 12–13.

Tu gardes contact avec les copains?

Comment? Par email? MSN? SMS?

Voir page 14.

Premiers contacts

Florian, 26 ans, moniteur

La colonie de vacances: travail ou vacances?

Voir pages 16–17.

Apprendre les mots nouveaux, c'est dur?

Tu oublies le vocabulaire?

Voir page 20.

Julien aime une fille mais ses copains la détestent. Qu'est-ce qu'il va faire?

Décide!

Voir page 22.

À la fin de l'unité 1, reviens ici et réponds aux questions!

En colonie de vacances

● Greetings and personal details

C'est le premier jour en colonie de vacances. On se fait des amis!

1 Regarde les photos A–E. Imagine. Qu'est-ce qu'ils disent?

Exemple *Bonjour! Salut! Ça va? Oui, et toi? Je m'appelle...*

A

B

C

D

E

Tu t'appelles comment?	**Je m'appelle** (Julien).
	Moi, c'est (Laura).
C'est qui?	**Voici** (mon copain / ma copine).
	Je suis (français(e)).
Tu parles quelles langues?	**Je parle** (anglais).
Tu viens d'où?	**Je viens de** (Marseille, en France).
Tu habites où?	**J'habite à** (Paris).
Tu as quel âge?	**J'ai... ans.**
C'est quand ton anniversaire?	**Mon anniversaire, c'est le** (21 janvier).

Grammaire

être *(to be)*
je suis, tu es, il/elle/on est

*Tu **es** français?*
Are you French?

avoir *(to have)*
j'ai, tu as, il/elle/on a

*Il **a** 16 ans.*
He **is** 16 years old.

Visit

2 Écoute et lis (1–5, page 11). Relie les conversations
et les photos.

1
- Salut! Je m'appelle Julien. Comment tu t'appelles?
- Salut! Moi, c'est Marc. Tu es français?
- Non, je suis suisse!
- Tu parles quelles langues?
- Français, allemand et anglais.

 2
- Tu viens d'où, Laura?
- Je viens d'Angleterre. Je suis anglaise.
- Tu habites où?
- À York. Et toi, Erwan?
- Moi, j'habite en Bretagne, dans le nord-ouest de la France.

3
- Tu as quel âge, Sophie?
- Treize ans. Et toi?
- Moi aussi*, mais toi, Sophie, tu es beaucoup plus grande que moi!   * me too.
- C'est quand ton anniversaire? Moi, c'est le 2 septembre.
- Moi, mon anniversaire, c'est le 21 juillet.

 3 Lis les conversations. Note les questions et donne l'équivalent anglais.

Exemple *Comment tu t'appelles?* = What's your name?

 4 Trouve les expressions qui répondent aux questions.

 5 À trois: complétez la conversation avec les expressions de la boîte (page 10).

Ben: Salut! [1] Ben. Et vous?
Éric: Salut Ben! [2] Éric. Et [3] ma copine, Lisa.
Lisa: Salut Ben! Tu es français?
Ben: Non, [4] anglais. [5] de Londres. Et toi, Lisa?
Lisa: Moi, [4] italienne. [6] à Rome. [7] un peu le français.
Ben: Tu parles super bien le français, Lisa!
Éric: Tu as quel âge, Ben?
Ben: [8] 14 [8]. Et toi?
Éric: Moi aussi. [9] 23 février.
Ben: C'est quand, ton anniversaire, Lisa?
Lisa: Le 4 août.
Ben: Moi aussi! C'est incroyable!! On fait la fête, d'accord?
Éric: OK, OK, viens, Lisa. Salut, Ben!

 6 Écoutez et vérifiez!

 Visit

Tu veux venir avec moi?

● Asking someone out; saying yes or no

Après-midi libre à la colonie...

Tu viens à la fête du village avec moi?

Non, désolée, je ne peux pas. Je vais à la piscine.

Dommage!*

Tu viens manger une glace avec moi?

Dommage!*   * Pity.

Non, désolée, je ne peux pas. J'ai mal aux dents!

Euh... non, désolé, Jojo. Je n'aime pas aller à la plage.

Salut, Max! Tu veux venir à la plage avec moi?

Vous venez au ciné avec moi?

Dommage!*

Non, désolée, on ne peut pas. On va à la crêperie.

Salut, Max! Tu veux venir à la plage avec moi?

Oui! Je veux bien! J'adore ça!

Génial!!!

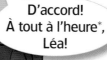

Super! On se retrouve à 13 heures dans le hall?

D'accord! À tout à l'heure*, Léa!   * See you later

13 heures...

 Lis et écoute. Trouve:

a   how to ask someone out (2 ways)
b   how to say you can't go
c   how to accept an offer or an invitation
d   how to arrange a time and place to meet

 Écris une liste des sorties mentionées dans l'histoire.

Exemple   *aller à la fête du village...*

Visit Clic! OxBox

Tu veux venir avec moi?

Grammaire

venir   *to come*

je	tu	il/elle/on
viens	**viens**	**vient**

Magali **vient** à la plage.
Magali is coming to the beach.

Magali, **1** à la piscine avec moi?

Euh... **2** J'ai mal à la jambe.

J'ai une idée! **3** manger une crêpe avec moi?

4 J'adore ça! **5** à 17 heures à la crêperie?

3 Complète les bulles avec les expressions à droite.

4 Écoute pour vérifier.

5 À deux: inventez et écrivez des conversations. (B→A)

A choisit une activité (page 12).
B lance le dé pour répondre:
1, 3, 5 = Oui; 2, 4, 6 = Non.

Exemple   **A** *Tu veux venir à la fête du village?*

B *Non, désolé(e), je ne peux pas.*
Je n'aime pas les fêtes.

Tu viens	à la	piscine
Tu veux venir	au	fête du village
		plage
		ciné(ma)
		bowling
manger (une glace)		

Non, désolé(e).
Désolé(e), je ne peux pas.
D'accord.
Oui, je veux bien.
On se retrouve à (17) heures?

Et après?

● Keeping in touch with friends

Tu gardes contact avec tes copains ou copines de vacances?

1 Au camp de vacances...

● je me fais un bon copain / une bonne copine.

■ je sors toujours avec les mêmes copains.

▲ je parle à tout le monde*!

* everybody

2 Les copains de vacances...

● je ne les revois jamais.

■ je les revois aux prochaines vacances.

▲ je les invite à mes fêtes.

* I lose touch with them.

Quand je rentre de vacances...

● je ne réponds pas toujours.

■ je prends contact avec une ou deux copains.

▲ je téléphone à mes nouveaux copains tous les jours.

3 Comment gardes-tu contact avec les copains?

● Je ne garde pas contact.

■ J'écris des emails, des SMS ou je téléphone.

▲ Je communique avec mes copains sur Facebook.

Résultats

Une majorité de:

● Tu dois être plus sociable!

■ Tu gardes contact avec tes copains, c'est bien!

▲ Tu ne peux pas garder contact avec tout le monde. Tu dois choisir!

---

1 Lis le jeu-test. L'image illustre quelle phrase?

Exemple *1* = ☐ , ...

Yann et Magali... à suivre*!

* to be continued

**C'est la fin des vacances.
Magali écrit un email à Yann.**

Salut, Yann!

Ça va? J'ai adoré les vacances! Je voudrais retourner en colonie, pas toi? ;-)

Dommage, les vacances sont finies! Demain, je dois retourner au collège! :-(

Je voudrais vraiment te revoir. Tu veux passer un week-end chez moi? Tu peux si tu veux, mes parents sont d'accord. :-) Demande à tes parents si tu peux venir et réponds-moi vite!

Bisous

Magali

P.S. Anya te dit bonjour!

 2 Lis l'email de Magali. Trouve le français.

a I would like to go back to summer camp.
b I have to go back to school.
c I would really like to see you again.
d Would you like to come to my place for a weekend?
e You can if you want to.
f Ask your parents if you can come.

 3 Yann téléphone à Magali. Écoute et choisis le bon verbe.

a Magali ★ revoir Yann pendant les vacances d'octobre.
b Il ★ bien aller chez elle mais il ne ★ pas.
c Il ★ aller en Angleterre avec sa classe.
d Il ne ★ pas aller en Angleterre.
e Il ★ aller chez Magali le premier week-end de novembre.
f Ses parents disent qu'il ★ .

 4 Tu invites un copain / une copine pour le week-end.
Invente une conversation au téléphone ou par MSN.

Exemple   **A** *Allô, Anya? Ici Magali.*
          B *Allô? Magali! Salut! Ça va?*
          A *Oui, super! Yann vient chez moi en novembre.
                 Tu veux venir passer un week-end chez moi?*
          B *Oui, mais je dois demander à mes parents.*
          A *D'accord. Tu peux rester le dimanche si tu veux.*
          B *Super, je veux bien.*

Grammaire

verbs + infinitive

	je	tu	il/elle/on
I have to	**dois**	**dois**	**doit**
I can	**peux**	**peux**	**peut**
I want to	**veux**	**veux**	**veut**
I would	**voudrais**	**voudrais**	like to

Je veux te revoir.
I want to see you again.

peut   veut   voudrait   doit

C'est la vie!

Florian Galera a 26 ans. Il habite à Aubagne.
Il est moniteur dans un centre aéré et dans une colonie de vacances.

Aubagne est une jolie ville.

Moniteur, c'est un travail sympa.

Florian aime travailler au centre aéré.

Les enfants ne s'amusent avec Florian.

VIDEO
1 Watch the video on Florian. Do you agree with the sentences on the right?

VIDEO
2a Put the sentences below in the order of the video clip.

a   What do you need to work at a holiday camp?
b   Do you like working in an after school club?
c   What do you do on a holiday camp?
d   What would you like to do later on?
e   How long have you been a youth leader?

VIDEO
3 Relie les réponses de Florian (1–5) aux questions (a–e). Regarde et vérifie.

1   J'aime travailler dans le centre aéré.
2   Je suis moniteur de colonie de vacances depuis cinq ans.
3   Il faut un diplôme qui s'appelle le BAFA.
4   Si c'est à la mer, nous allons faire de la plongée, etc. En montagne, on fait de l'escalade, etc.
5   Je voudrais devenir directeur de mon centre.

Le sais-tu?

● Many young French people prepare for the *BAFA* (*brevet d'aptitude aux fonctions d'animateur*) to be able to work in youth centres and summer camps.
● Most French towns have a *centre aéré*. Typical opening hours are weekdays 7.30–19.00.

Visit **clic!** [O:Box]

Florian aime le métier de moniteur...

4 Complète la légende de la photo. Ton / Ta partenaire est d'accord?

a ... parce qu'il aime le sport.
b ... parce que ce n'est pas fatigant.
c ... parce qu'il aime s'amuser.

5 Read the card on the qualities needed to be a youth leader. Match the categories 1–3 to the qualities a–h.

1 the role of a youth leader (3 points)
2 the qualities of a youth leader (4 points)
3 the advantage of speaking a foreign language for a youth leader (1 point)

Moniteur / Monitrice

a aimer les enfants
b s'occuper* des enfants
c avoir de l'énergie
d animer* des activités
e aimer les activités sportives
f être sociable et patient
g organiser des jeux
h travailler dans des colonies de vacances à l'étranger

*to look after
to lead

Grammaire

In French, to say how long or since when you've been doing something, use a present tense + *depuis*:

Il est moniteur depuis 2007.
= He **has been** a youth leader **since** 2007.

Il travaille ici depuis un mois.
= He **has been** working here **for** a month.

6 Tu aimerais être moniteur / monitrice de colonie? Pourquoi? Utilise les points **a–h** et / ou des raisons personnelles.

Exemple *J'aimerais être moniteur/monitrice parce que j'aime les enfants, etc.*

ou

 Je n'aimerais pas être moniteur/monitrice parce que je n'aime pas organiser des jeux, etc...

7a Grammaire: écoute et complète les phrases.

Exemple *1 Il habite ici depuis un mois.*

2 Il est moniteur au centre aéré depuis...
3 Il parle espagnol depuis...
4 Il a le BAFA depuis...

All about verbs

How much do you know about French verbs?

Look at a–h. Are you familiar with them?

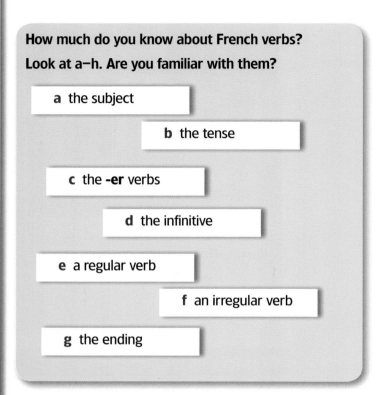

a the subject

b the tense

c the **-er** verbs

d the infinitive

e a regular verb

f an irregular verb

g the ending

1 Match **1–8** with **a–h** to complete the definitions.

1 is the part of the verb meaning 'to...' , as found in a dictionary.

2 are the largest group of verbs in French.

3 indicates who is doing the 'action' described by the verb.

4 shows whether it's present, past or future.

5 is the part of the verb that changes with the subject.

6 follows the same pattern as others in its group.

7 doesn't follow a pattern and needs to be learned by heart.

Verbs in the present tense

In French, use the present tense to say:

A what you are doing right now

Je mange. Il regarde la télé.
I am eating. He's watching TV.

B what you do generally / routinely / regularly

Je mange à 12 h 30. Il regarde la télé tous les soirs.
I eat at 12.30. He watches TV every evening.

2a Match these sentences to definitions **A–B**.

1 Je pars en vacances tous les ans.

2 Je vais à la piscine une fois par semaine.

3 Il va en colonie de vacances en juillet.

4 – Tu viens?
– Non, je mange.

5 Qu'est-ce que tu fais?

6 On arrive!

7 Je vais au collège à huit heures.

8 Je retrouve mes copains le samedi.

2b Translate sentences **1–8** into English.

Visit **Clic!**

Regular and irregular verbs

1 Most verbs ending in **-er** are regular (except **aller**):

jouer:	je	jou**e**
	tu	jou**es**
	il/elle/on	jou**e**
	nous	jou**ons**
	vous	jou**ez**
	ils/elles	jou**ent**

2 The most common irregular verbs are **être** and **avoir** and you need to know them by heart. With other irregular verbs, endings still follow a recognisable pattern.

	avoir	être
j'/je	ai	suis
tu	as	es
il/elle/on	a	est
nous	avon	sommes
vous	avez	êtes
il/elles	ont	sont

3 Write out each sentence using the correct form of the verb in brackets.

a On [**rester**] à la maison cet été.

b Tu [**aimer**] partir en vacances?

c Vous [**envoyer**] souvent des emails?

d Nous [**adorer**] le français.

e Il [**regarder**] toujours la télé!

f Ils [**manger**] avec des copains ce soir.

g Elles [**commencer**] les cours à dix-sept heures.

h Je [**renter**] à la maison tard le soir.

4 Copy and complete these present tense verbs.

a je chant∗∗, je regard∗∗, je mang∗∗

b tu mang∗∗, tu arriv∗∗, tu invit∗∗

c il parl∗∗, elle retrouv∗∗, on ador∗∗

d nous aim∗∗, nous détest∗∗, nous voul∗∗

e vous regard∗∗, vous mang∗∗, vous trouv∗∗

f ils téléphon∗∗, ils parl∗∗, elles rest∗∗

5 Check how well you know **avoir** and **être**: choose a verb, your partner chooses a subject pronoun (*je*, *tu*, etc.) − write it down with the correct verb.

I find learning new words and phrases quite difficult. What is the best way to do it?

I keep forgetting the words I've learned! What can I do?

The golden rule is: revise and reuse often.

- Write the words in a notebook and record them on your MP3 or mobile.

- Concentrate on words you find difficult: write a cue (English translation) on sticky labels and fix them to your bedroom door.

- Look at new words at regular intervals: daily at first, then weekly and monthly once you know them better.

Learning vocabulary takes time and practice. Try out various strategies and see which suits you best.

- Say (or sing or chant) and listen to the words (recorded on MP3 / mobile)

- If you're more visual, then mime, write or draw the words.

- Associate words or phrases with mental images that are meaningful to you (teeth = *les dents* → dentist)

- Write words on cards. On the back write a translation or definition or draw a picture. Then play games like *Match the pairs* or *Snap*.

1a **Choose a few strategies from above and learn this list of words from unit 1.**

les dents   fatigant   ensemble   tout le monde   dommage   moniteur   perdre de vue

1b **Compare your strategies with your partner. Which method did you find the easiest?**

2 **Make a poster. Write the words you want to learn on sticky notes and stick them in the Daily column.**

Daily	Weekly	Monthly
les dents		
fatigant		

a After a day, move the words you know to the Weekly column.
b After a week, move those you know to the Monthly column. Those you don't know go back to the Daily column.
c After a month, remove those you know. Those you don't know go back to the Weekly column... and so on!

Visit

Tu sais tout?

Écoute!

1 Listen to Magali and Anya. Answer *yes, no* **or** *maybe* **to each question.**

1 Magali invites Anya to her house?
2 Anya can go to Magali's?
3 She wants to go to the wedding?
4 Anya will talk to her parents.
5 Her parents say yes?

Lis!

2 Read the postcard Magali wrote to a friend while at summer camp. Number these sentences in the right order (1–6) to summarise the text.

Example *1 = e*

a She didn't like camp at first.
b She's met a boy through a friend, Anya.
c She can't wait to go out with Yann tonight.
d She'd love to go out with Yann.
e She has never been to a camp before.
f She was feeling homesick.

Salut Morgane!

Je suis en colonie de vacances. C'est la première fois! Au début, c'était nul parce que je ne connaissais personne. J'ai passé des heures au téléphone avec ma mère! Mais maintenant, je suis copine avec Anya, une fille très sympa. En plus, ce matin, Anya m'a présenté un garçon génial! Il s'appelle Yann. Il est adorable.
Je voudrais bien sortir avec lui. ;-)

Je t'embrasse

Magali

P.S. Yann m'a invitée à sortir avec lui ce soir!
On va manger des crêpes au village.

Écris!

3 Write a paragraph about yourself, giving the following information.

Example *Je m'appelle Kieron Langley.*
    or: *Moi, c'est Kieron Langley.*

- name, age and birthday
- where you live
- where you are from
- whether you enjoyed your last holiday, and what in particular
- nationality; languages spoken

Parle!

4 You are being asked out. Read the questions, look at the picture cues and give your answers.

Example *a Non, désolé(e), je ne peux pas. Je vais à la piscine.*

a Tu viens à la plage avec moi? ✗

b Tu viens manger une glace? ✗

c Tu viens manger une crêpe? ✗

d Alors, tu veux venir au cinéma? ✗

e Tu veux faire du vélo avec moi? ✓

f Super! On se retrouve où et quand?

À tout à l'heure!

Quel dilemme!

Amélie n'aime pas la colonie. Les filles parlent de mode ou jouent au foot avec les garçons. Nul!
Tous se moquent* d'elle parce qu'elle est différente. Sa grande passion, c'est le piano. Alors, Amélie est souvent seule. Elle joue sur le piano du salon.

* make fun of.

«Julien, on a temps libre.
Tu joues au foot?» demande Luc, un des copains de Julien.
«Euh, non... je vais au salon.
Vous venez?» répond Julien.
«Ah non! Miss Beethoven est au piano, beurk!
Je déteste cette fille», répond Luc.

Julien entre au salon. Il regarde Amélie. Il va se moquer d'elle?
«Je peux jouer du piano avec toi?» demande Julien, doucement.
«Euh... oui...!» répond Amélie. Julien est sympa.
 Elle est contente.
«Tu veux venir à la fête du village ce soir?» demande Julien.
Amélie ne répond pas... c'est vraiment un rêve!

Les copains de Julien arrivent au salon.
Julien parle avec ses copains.
«Tu viens au village ce soir?» demande Luc.
«Euh... oui, avec Amélie», répond Julien.
«Quoi? Ah non, elle est nulle, cette fille. C'est nous ou elle. Tu comprends?»

Julien aime bien ses copains mais ses copains détestent Amélie. C'est dommage! Il aime beaucoup Amélie.
Qu'est-ce qu'il va faire?

 1a Before reading, look at the illustrations. What do you think the story is about?

 1b Read the story. Answer in English.

 a Where does the story take place?

 b Who is the story about?

 c What happens?

 d What is the dilemma?

 2 Read the advice on the right. Which of Julien's friends do you think gives him the best advice?

Clément: «Garde tes copains et ne sors pas avec cette fille. Les copains sont plus importants!»

Léandre: «Sors avec tes copains, mais invente une excuse polie pour Amélie.»

Laura: «Sors avec Amélie en secret, ne dis rien à tes copains!»

Estelle: «Si tu as envie de sortir avec Amélie, sors avec elle. Tu fais comme tu veux.»

Visit **Clic!**

clic-mag

Attention, danger!

L'histoire vraie d'Antoine, 14 ans

Le web, c'est super! On peut discuter avec d'autres jeunes dans les chat-rooms. Mais il faut faire attention!

1 «Samedi dernier, après mon match de foot, un homme arrive en voiture. Il me dit: «Salut! Tu es Antoine, non? Tu joues bien au foot!» On parle de foot. Il dit: «Monte dans la voiture!» Il est vraiment sympa, alors je monte.

2 On s'arrête sur un parking. Il met sa main sur ma jambe... Brrrr! Je panique! Je sors de la voiture. Je crie et l'homme part.

3 Je rentre à la maison et je dis tout à mes parents. Ils demandent:
«Tu parles à qui sur le web?»

Alors, je me rappelle un garçon de mon âge dans la chat-room.
Il adore le foot. Avec lui, on discute du match de samedi. Il demande comment je suis physiquement: il veut me voir sur le terrain.
En fait, l'homme de la voiture, c'est lui... »

**Tu es dans une chat-room.
Tu réponds ou pas?**

▶ Quels sont tes passe-temps préférés?

▶ Tu peux sortir le week-end?

▶ On se retrouve au fast-food?

▶ Tu veux être dans un petit film?

▶ Tu aimes quelle musique?

▶ Tu as quel âge?

▶ C'est quoi, ton numéro de portable?

▶ Tu me donnes ton adresse email et je t'envoie des photos de ta star préférée?

▶ Tu es comment physiquement?

▶ Comment tu t'appelles?

---

 1 Before reading the article, guess what it is about. What helps you?

 2a Read *L'histoire vraie de...* Match illustrations A–C to paragraphs 1–3.

 2b Find the French phrases for sentences a–h and put them in the right order.

a After my football game, a man arrives in a car.
b I shout and the man leaves.
c He says 'Get into the car!'
d I remember a boy my age in the chatroom.

e We stop at a car park.
f He puts his hand on my leg.
g I tell my parents everything.
h He asks what I look like.

 3 Read *Tu es dans une chat-room*. Work out what the questions mean. Would you answer them in a chatroom? Discuss in English.

Vocabulaire

Premières rencontres

First encounters

Comment tu t'appelles?

What's your name?

Je m'appelle X.

My name is X.

Et toi?

What about you?

Moi, c'est Y.

I'm Y.

Tu es français(e)?

Are you French?

Je suis anglais(e) / britannique.

I'm English / British.

Tu parles quelles langues?

What languages do you speak?

Je parle anglais et français.

I speak English and French.

Tu viens d'où?

Where do you come from?

Je viens de Grande-Bretagne.

I come from Britain.

Tu habites où?

Where do you live?

J'habite à Glasgow.

I live in Glasgow.

Tu as quel âge?

How old are you?

J'ai 13 ans.

I'm 13.

C'est quand ton anniversaire?

When's your birthday?

C'est le 21 mai.

It's on May 21st.

Je te présente X. / Voici X.

This is X.

Salut! Bonjour!

Hi! Hello!

Tu es déjà venu(e) ici?

Have you been here before?

Non, c'est la première fois.

No, it's my first time.

Je suis venu(e) l'année dernière.

I came last year.

Sortir

Going out

Tu viens [à la fête] avec moi?

(to one person) Are you coming [to the fête] with me?

Vous venez [au ciné] avec moi?

(to several people) Are you coming [to the cinema] with me?

Tu veux venir [à la plage] avec moi?

Do you want to come to the beach with me?

Non, désolé(e), je ne peux pas.

No, sorry, I can't.

Je vais à la piscine.

I'm going to the swimming pool.

J'ai mal aux dents.

I have toothache.

On ne peut pas.

We can't.

On va à la crêperie.

We're going to the pancake restaurant.

Dommage!

Shame!/What a pity!

Oui! Je veux bien!

Yes. I'd like/love to!

J'adore ça!

I love that!

On se retrouve ici à X heures?

Shall we meet here at X o'clock?

D'accord.

OK.

À tout à l'heure.

See you later.

Garder contact

Keeping in touch

un copain / une copine

a friend

Je ne réponds pas toujours.

I don't always reply.

Je téléphone tous les jours.

I phone everyday.

J'envoie des emails.

I send emails.

J'envoie des SMS.

I text.

Je communique sur Facebook.

I communicate on Facebook.

Premier email après la rencontre

First email after meeting

Dommage, les vacances sont finies!

Shame, the holiday's over!

Je dois retourner au collège.

I have to go back to school.

J'ai adoré mes vacances avec toi.

I loved my holidays with you.

Je voudrais te revoir!

I want to see you again!

Tu veux passer un week-end chez moi?

Would you like to come to my place for a weekend?

Mes parents sont d'accord.

My parents are OK with it.

Demande à tes parents.

Ask your parents.

Réponds-moi vite!

Answer / Write back quickly!

Je t'embrasse.

Love from...

Bisous.

Love from...

Le travail de moniteur	**_Working as a camp leader_**
un moniteur / une monitrice	_youth leader_
un centre aéré	_after school club_
une colonie de vacances	_a holiday camp_
Qu'est-ce qu'il faut...?	_What do you need...?_
Il faut avoir / être...	_You need to have / to be..._
sociable / patient	_sociable / patient_
Qu'est-ce que vous voudriez faire plus tard?	_What would you like to do later on?_
Je voudrais devenir...	_I'd like to become..._
Depuis combien de temps?	_For how long?_
un diplôme	_a diploma_

une formation	_training_
s'occuper d'enfants	_to look after children_
animer des activités	_to lead activities_
Il est moniteur depuis 2007.	_He's been a leader since 2007._
Il travaille ici depuis un mois.	_He's been working here for one month._

 Make up as many sentences as you can about the pictures using the words / phrases on this page.

Pourquoi apprendre le français?

Pour parler de choses intéressantes avec des amis francophones

Voir page 28.

Tu regardes souvent la télé?
Quelle est ton émission préférée?

Tu aimes regarder les infos?

NOUS FAISONS PEUR
ET NOUS LE FAISONS BIEN

Par les créateurs de TOY STORY

Disney·PIXAR
MONSTRES & Cie
www.disney.fr

Ton acteur préféré, c'est qui?
Et ton actrice préférée?

Tu aimes quel genre de film?

Voir page 30.

Voir page 40.

Je vais manquer une fête familiale importante pour aller à un match de foot.

C'est le bon choix?
Décide!

À mon avis 2

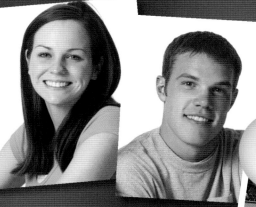

Charlotte est sportive?
Jérémy a regardé quels
sports?

Voir page 32.

Tu as des problèmes pour
comprendre le français?

On parle trop vite?

Voir page 38.

Charlie, 16 ans. Lycéen ou
basketteur professionnel?

Lundi matin au lycée, il
est fatigué.

Pourquoi?

Voir page 34.

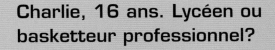

À la fin de l'unité 2, reviens ici et
réponds aux questions!

C'est nul, ça!

● TV programmes and your opinion of them

 1 **Relie.**

Exemple *1 b*

a	un dessin animé
b	un documentaire
c	une émission de télé réalité
d	une émission musicale
e	une émission sportive
f	un feuilleton
g	un film
h	les informations
i	un jeu télévisé

2 **Regarde les photos. Écoute et note les émissions de télé dans l'ordre. Quelle émission n'est pas mentionnée?**

Exemple *un feuilleton*

3a **Écoute (1–8). C'est positif** **, négatif** **u entre les deux** **?**

3b **Réécoute (1–8) et note les opinions (a–o).**

Exemple *1,*  *k (déteste), m (nul)*

😊		😐		☹️	
a j'adore		**h** bof, pas mal		**j** je n'aime pas (du tout)	
b j'aime bien		**i** ça va, mais...		**k** je déteste	
c je préfère				**l** j'ai horreur de / des...	
c'est	**d** marrant			c'est	**m** nul
	e génial				**n** trop bête
	f super				**o** ennuyeux
	g intéressant				

4 À deux: posez une question sur chaque genre d'émission de télé

Exemple **A** *Comment tu trouves les feuilletons?*

B *Ah, c'est nul! Je déteste les feuilletons!*
Et toi, tu aimes ça?

A *Bof, pas mal. C'est assez intéressant...*

To emphasise your opinion:
très = *very*
assez = *quite*
trop = *too*

5 Lis l'email. Recopie et corrige les phrases a–e.

Défi!

Draw up your ideal TV schedule for one day. Ask your partner for his/her opinion.

Salut, Léa!

Moi, j'aime bien regarder la télé. J'aime bien les films et les feuilletons, mais je n'aime pas les jeux télévisés – c'est nul! Mon émission préférée, c'est "Friends" – c'est assez vieux, mais c'est marrant. Je regarde ça souvent avec ma copine.
Mon frère, Daniel, adore les émissions de télé réalité, comme "On a échangé nos mamans" – il trouve ça génial et c'est son émission préférée. Il déteste les informations parce que c'est trop long. Moi non plus, je n'aime pas ça. C'est ennuyeux.
Et toi? Qu'est-ce que tu aimes regarder à la télé?
Écris-moi vite!

Mathilde

Mathilde

a Mathilde's favourite TV programmes are about sports.

b She often watches her favourite programme with her brother.

c *On a échangé nos mamans* is a cartoon.

d Her brother hates reality shows.

e Her friend hates the TV series *Friends*.

6 Réécris l'email pour toi. Change les mots soulignés.

7 Fais un sondage en classe.

Quelle est ton émission préférée?	*Mon émission préférée, c'est "EastEnders".*
C'est quelle sorte d'émission?	*C'est un feuilleton.*
Qu'est-ce que tu n'aimes pas?	*Je déteste les émissions sportives.*
Pourquoi?	*C'est ennuyeux.*

Grammaire

Possessive adjectives
The words for 'my', 'your', 'his' and 'her' agree with the noun they belong to, masculine, feminine or plural:

English	m. sing.	f. sing.	plural
my	mon	ma	mes
your	ton	ta	tes
his/her	son	sa	ses

Remember: **son / sa / ses** mean 'his' or 'her'.

8 Résume les préférences d'une personne avec qui tu as discuté. Lis à la classe qui devine qui c'est.

Exemple *Il / Elle adore / déteste les feuilletons. Son émission préférée, c'est East Enders.*

Au grand écran

● Discussing films; describing the plot and characters of a film

 Regarde le programme. C'est quel genre de film?

Exemple *1 – e un film de guerre*

a	**une comédie**
b	**un dessin animé**
c	**un film d'action**
d	**un film d'amour**
e	**un film de guerre**
f	**un film d'horreur**
g	**un film de science-fiction**

Ciné-club

1 Il faut sauver le soldat Ryan

2 Mission Impossible 3

5 Shrek le Troisième

 Écoute le répondeur du Ciné-club et vérifie.

3 La Guerre des Étoiles

4 Un homme et une femme

2 **Écoute Chloé et choisis ses réponses aux questions.**

1 Tu aimes quel genre de film?
  a les films de science-fiction
  b les comédies

2 Quel est ton film préféré?
  a *La Guerre des Mondes*
  b *La Guerre des Étoiles*

3 Qui est ton acteur préféré?
  a Tom Cruise **b** Orlando Bloom

4 Pourquoi?
  a il est talentueux **b** il est beau et romantique

5 Qui est ton actrice préférée?
  a Julie Delpy **b** Juliette Binoche

6 Pourquoi?
  a elle est belle **b** elle est très intelligente et talentueuse

6 Entretien avec un vampire

7 Les vacances de Mr Bean

3 **À deux: A pose les questions 1–6 et B répond. (B→A) Utilise des adjectifs de la boîte.**

beau / **belle**	**mince**
grand / **grande**	**drôle**
naturel / **naturelle**	**romantique**
amusant / **amusante**	**sympa**
intelligent / **intelligente**	
talentueux / **talentueuse**	

4 **Grammaire: trouve six autres adjectifs pour décrire ton acteur préféré / actrice préférée (3 pour son physique et 3 pour sa personnalité). Attention aux accords masculins / féminins!**

Visit Clic! OxBox

Les Pirates des Caraïbes: la Malédiction du Black Pearl, c'est un film d'action et une comédie. C'est avec Johnny Depp, Orlando Bloom et Keira Knightley.

C'est l'histoire d'un pirate un peu fou, Jack Sparrow, et de deux jeunes amoureux, Will Smith et Elizabeth.

Moi, j'ai adoré ce film parce que c'était super drôle et passionnant! Les acteurs étaient géniaux et les effets spéciaux aussi!

À mon avis, c'est un film à voir!

 5 Lis le commentaire de Chloé sur *Pirates des Caraïbes*. Réponds.

    a C'est quel genre de film?
    b C'est avec qui?
    c C'est comment?

 6 Écoute Luc parler du film, *le Fils du Mask*. Réponds aux questions a–c.

 7a À deux: choisissez un film que vous avez vu récemment.

    A Tu as vu…?   **B** Non, je n'ai pas vu… / Oui, je l'ai vu.

 7b Écris un commentaire sur ce film. Utilise les expressions de la boîte.

C'est un film d'action / une comédie.
C'est avec…
J'ai beaucoup aimé (ce film) parce que…
Je n'ai pas beaucoup aimé (ce film) parce que…

Les acteurs étaient nuls / géniaux.
Les effets spéciaux étaient nuls / géniaux.
C'était long / ennuyeux.
C'était drôle / passionnant.
C'est un film à voir. ✓ ✓
C'est un film à éviter. ✗ ✗

Le sport en rêve

● Talking about sports

Charlotte et Jérémy rêvent...

En automne, j'étais en France pour la Coupe du Monde.

En été, j'étais aux 24 h du Mans. C'était extraordinaire!

En hiver, j'étais dans les Alpes pour le championnat du monde. Le ski, j'adore ça!

Au printemps, j'étais à Paris pour la finale de la Ligue des Champions. C'était fantastique!

1 **Regarde les photos A–E. C'est quel sport?**

le ski   le football
le rugby   la Formule 1
le roller

2a **Écoute (1–4) et trouve la bonne photo.**

Exemple *1 A*

2b **Réécoute Charlotte et Jérémy: joueur / joueuse, arbitre, entraîneur / entraîneuse ou spectateur / spectatrice?**

Exemple *1 arbitre*

À deux. Jeu de mémoire: reliez les saisons et les sports (photos A–E).

3 Exemple **A** *En automne...*
         B *Le rugby?*
         A *Oui.*

les quatre saisons	les sportifs
en automne	arbitre
en hiver	entraîneur / entraîneuse
au printemps	joueur / joueuse
en été	spectateur / spectatrice

Visit cJic! OxBox

4 À deux: devinez − Charlotte ou Jérémy?

Exemple **A** *C'était fantastique!* **B** *C'était en été?*
 A *Non.* **B** *C'était au printemps?*
 A *Oui.* **B** *Tu étais spectateur?*
 A *Non.* **B** *Tu étais arbitre?*
 A *Oui.* **B** *Tu es Jérémy!*
 A *Oui.*

> c'était (en été / au printemps etc.) = *it was*
> j'étais (spectateur / joueur / arbitre) = *I was*
> tu étais (spectateur / joueur / arbitre) = *you were*

5 Trouve l'entraîneur, le joueur, le spectateur et l'arbitre.

a J'ai participé au match, mais je n'étais pas joueur.

b Je n'ai pas participé au championnat, mais j'ai fait du ski.

c J'ai participé, mais je n'étais pas arbitre.

d Je n'ai pas participé, mais j'ai assisté au match.

Grammaire

Verb tenses

present	perfect	perfect + negative
je joue *(I play)*	j'ai joué *(I played)*	je n'ai pas joué *(I didn't play)*
je fais *(I do)*	j'ai fait *(I did)*	je n'ai pas fait *(I didn't do)*
je participe *(I take part)*	j'ai participé *(I took part)*	je n'ai pas participé *(I didn't take part)*
j'assiste *(I watch)*	j'ai assisté *(I watched)*	je n'ai pas assisté *(I didn't watch)*

6 À toi. Imagine que tu es fanatique d'un sport: remplace les mots soulignés.

present:

a Je suis vraiment fanatique de snowboard.

 d'athlétisme d'alpinisme de gymnastique de natation

b C'est extraordinaire comme sport!

 fantastique super passionnant

c Normalement, je fais du snowboard en hiver. J'adore ça!

 en automne en été au printemps

perfect:

d L'année dernière,...

 la semaine dernière en janvier en février en septembre

e J'ai participé à la finale de la Coupe du Monde de snowboard.

 au championnat (du monde) de à la finale de la Coupe du Monde de

f J'ai fini en deuxième position.

 j'ai gagné la deuxième / troisième / dernière position

C'est la vie! 🎥

READING

1 **Choisis deux ou trois opinions pour toi.**

> Moi aussi, je suis passionné/e de sport.

> Je n'aime pas les sportifs.

> Charlie est sympa.

> Je ne joue pas au basket mais j'aimerais aller à Seattle, USA!

> Je déteste le sport, mais j'aime bien les clubs.

Voici Charlie. Il joue au basket-ball depuis 13 ans. Il habite à Marseille.

READING

2 **Lis a–c et complète les phrases avec les mots à droite. Regarde le clip et vérifie.**

a Alors, je m' ① Charlie et ② 16 ans.

b Ma passion ③ le ④ . J' ⑤ ça.

c J'avais 3 ans quand j'ai ⑥ à jouer.

> basket-ball

> commencé · adore · c'est · appelle · j'ai

VIDEO

3a **Regarde la première partie de l'interview et mets les photos et les extraits dans l'ordre du clip.**

A

B

C LIGUE NATIONALE DES JUNIORS DE BASKETBALL
Tournoi* international
JSA, BORDEAUX (F) contre TOULON (F) et HOUSTON (USA)
dim. 3 octobre, 14h à Fos-sur-Mer

Tu joues au basket en Ligue Nationale des Juniors?

D

Non, je joue au basket en Ligue de Championnat de France, en Cadets Division 2.

Des fois* je parle anglais quand je joue au basket mais pas souvent.

*sometimes/occasionally

C'est **S**tade **M**arseillais **U**niversitaire **C**lub.

SPEAKING

3b **À deux: comment dit-on en anglais les phrases A–D?**

WRITING

4 **Regarde tes notes et complète les réponses de Charlie.**

> Tu peux m'expliquer ce que ça veut dire SMUC?
> C'est Stade…
> Alors, Charlie, tu joues au basket en Ligue Nationale des Juniors?
> Non, …
> Tu parles anglais aussi quand tu joues au basket?
> …mais pas souvent.

Visit **Clic!** OxBox

Le sais-tu?

- In France schools do not organise sports fixtures, including basketball, with other schools. Students must join local clubs instead.
- The FFBB (La Fédération Française de Basket-Ball) trains male and female basketball players for professional clubs and the clubs organise fixtures and tournaments.

5 Regarde le clip sur l'emploi du temps de Charlie dimanche dernier. Relie les photos (1–6) et les extraits (a–f).

a Je me suis couché.
b J'ai pris mon petit déjeuner.
c Je me suis levé.

d Vous vous êtes échauffés*?
e Je suis rentré à 10 h 30.
f Je me suis lavé.

*Did you warm up?

6 Lis le résumé de la visite de Charlie à Seattle. Corrige les deux erreurs.

> In Seattle it's very beautiful and there's a good atmosphere. Charlie loves that about it. He wasn't the only foreign student there playing basketball. There were lots of good players but overall it wasn't very enjoyable.

7 Lis la question et relie les phrases. Puis regarde le clip et vérifie.

Exemple A5

> Tu vas devenir professionnel un jour?

A Ah, ça, si c'est...
B Alors, moi, ...
C Parce que c'est le sport...
D Donc tu es toujours...
E Et ça, c'est vraiment...

1 ...le plus technique au monde, je pense.
2 ...obligé d'essayer de progresser, de progresser, de progresser*.
3 ...j'adore le basket.
4 ...excitant.
5 ...le destin*, j'espère.

*you always have to try to progress, progress, progress
destiny

Défi!

Et toi, tu es sportif / sportive? Tu vas devenir professionnel(le) un jour? Choisis ton sport et écris ta réponse. Donne tes raisons.

Exemple

Oui, je voudrais bien être...
J'adore... Ma passion, c'est... parce que...

Non, je ne voudrais pas être...
Je ne suis pas très... et je n'aime pas...
L'entraînement? C'est trop...

Labo-langue

The perfect tense – *le passé composé*

> Je suis fatiguée!

> Qu'est-ce que tu as fait?

> J'ai joué au tennis avec Julien, puis j'ai fait du shopping en ville. J'ai acheté de nouvelles baskets. Julien a vu un ballon de foot, mais c'était trop cher. Après ça, on a fait un petit tour de 20 kilomètres à vélo.

> Et toi, tu as fait beaucoup de choses?

> Ah oui, moi aussi, je suis fatigué...

> ... j'ai fini TROIS jeux vidéo!

- This is the main tense used to talk about what you **did** or **have done** in the past. It is made up of two parts, just like in English, 'I have' + 'played'. They are called: the **auxiliary** (have/has) + the **past participle** (played, travelled, etc.)

- Most verbs have *avoir* as the auxiliary, so you need to know *avoir* really well:

j'ai *joué*	**nous avons** *joué*
tu as *joué*	**vous avez** *joué*
il/elle/on a *joué*	**ils/elles ont** *joué*

- The pattern of <u>endings</u> for the past participle of **-er** verbs is:

  –er → **-é**   jou**er** → jou**é**

- Some verbs have irregular past participles that you need to learn by heart.

dire → **dit**	écrire → **écrit**	faire → **fait**
mettre → **mis**	prendre → **pris**	être → **été**
avoir → **eu**	voir → **vu**	

For the full list, see *Grammaire* page 137.

---

1 **Find the perfect tense verbs in the cartoon.**

Example *tu as fait*

2 **Write the correct past participle. Then choose the correct word to complete the English translation.**

Example **a** *Il a <u>joué</u> au tennis. He <u>played</u> tennis.*

a Il a [**jouer**] au tennis.   He ✳✳✳ tennis.

b J'ai [**manger**] trois glaces.   I've ✳✳✳ three ice creams.

c Tu as [**écouter**] un nouveau CD.   You ✳✳✳ a new CD.

d On a [**acheter**] le poster à 3€.   We have ✳✳✳ the poster for 3 euros.

e Nous avons [**prendre**] le bus.   We ✳✳✳ the bus.

f Vous avez [**participer**] au match?   Did you ✳✳✳ in the match?

g Ils ont [**mettre**] un sweat rouge.   They ✳✳✳ red sweatshirts.

---

bought   eaten   chose   played   took   play   put on

The perfect tense with *être*

- A group of common verbs use *être* as the auxiliary, instead of *avoir*. These verbs are mostly **to do with coming and going**: *aller, venir, arriver, partir, entrer, sortir, monter, descendre*. See *Grammaire* page 138. Obviously, you need to know *être* just as well as *avoir*:

je suis	**nous sommes**
tu es	**vous êtes**
il/elle/on est	**ils/elles sont**

- The past participle of verbs with *être* has to 'agree' with the subject (the person doing the verb). If the subject is feminine, add **-e**; if it's plural, add **-s**; if it's feminine <u>and</u> plural, add **-es**.

Je suis arrivé.
I arrived. (boy speaking)

Je suis arrivée.
I arrived. (girl speaking)

Luc est allé au match.
Luc went to the match.

Lucie est allée au match.
Lucie went to the match.

On est allés au match.
We went to the match.

On est all<u>és</u> au match.
We went to the match.

3 **Choose the correct words to complete the French sentences and the translations.**

Example a Je <u>suis</u> sorti de la maison à 8 heures.
I <u>left</u> home at 8 o'clock.

a Je ✳✳✳ sorti de la maison à 8 h 00.   *I ✳✳✳ home at 8 o'clock.*

b Elle est ✳✳✳ au cinéma.   *✳✳✳ went to the cinema.*

c ✳✳✳ est arrivée à 5 h 00.   *She ✳✳✳ at 5 o'clock.*

d Nathalie, tu es ✳✳✳ à la maison?   *Nathalie, ✳✳✳ you stay at home?*

e Le skieur ✳✳✳ descendu à toute vitesse.   *The skier came ✳✳✳ at full speed.*

f Marc est ✳✳✳ au concert avec son amie.   *Marc ✳✳✳ come to the concert with his girlfriend.*

venu	allée	suis
restée	sont	Elles

	down	arrived
left	did	has	She

4 **Write out the sentences, putting the verbs into the perfect tense. Watch out – there's a mixture of *avoir* and *être* verbs!**

Example a Nous avons voyagé avec l'équipe.
b Tu es descendu / descendue du podium.

a Nous [**voyager**] avec l'équipe.

b Tu [**aller**] sur le podium.

c Je [**regarder**] un très bon film.

d Il [**entrer**] pendant mon émission préférée.

e Élodie, tu [**sortir**] avec Luc?

f Pour aller à la fête, on [**prendre**] un taxi.

g Elle [**monter**] jusqu'en haut du stade.

A When people speak French, all the words seem to come out as one long sound and I can't understand what they're saying.

B Is there anything I can do to help with listening activities in class?

Sometimes French people speak quickly.

- Why not ask them (politely!) to speak more slowly?

→ *Parlez plus lentement, s'il vous plaît.*

→ *Je n'ai pas compris. Tu peux parler plus lentement, s'il te plaît?*

- Try to get the **general sense** of what someone is saying without having to understand every single word.

If you're doing a listening exercise, give yourself a head start by good **preparation**:

- Read the **questions** so you know what you have to do.
- Look at any **images** – they're there to help you.
- Read the **examples** – they provide clues.
- Try to **predict** the words you might hear.

  While you're listening, make **brief notes** – no sentences, just key words and phrases.

Listen to the tone of voice.

- **Intonation** is about the way the voice goes up and down. It can tell you whether someone is making a statement or asking a question.

  Matthieu a gagné. ⟶ *Matthew won.*

  Matthieu a gagné? ⟶ *Did Matthew win?*

 1 Listen and decide what each person (1–3) is talking about: horse racing, cycling or a soap opera.

 2 Listen (1–7): who is asking a question? Put a question mark if it's a question and a full stop if it's a statement.

 Écoute!
Listen to a conversation between Ludovic and Chris. Choose the right option for each sentence below: a, b or c.

1 On Saturday night, Ludovic...
   a went to the match.
   b went to the cinema.
   c went to London.

2 Laura comes from...
   a Leeds.
   b London.
   c Paris.

3 Chris watched telly...
   a Sunday evening.
   b Saturday morning.
   c Saturday evening.

4 Chris's evening was...
   a boring.
   b great.
   c extraordinary.

5 They...
   a lost 1–0.
   b won 3–0.
   c lost 3–0.

 Parle!
Choose two types of TV programmes that you like and two that you don't like. Give reasons.

Example *Alors, j'aime bien les feuilletons parce que... et... mais je déteste... parce que...*

 Imagine you love doing a sport: choose which one and imagine the details. Complete the sentences below and say them to your partner.

Je suis vraiment fanatique de... (quel sport?)
C'est... (c'est comment?)
Normalement.... (où? quand?)
L'année dernière, j'ai... je suis...
C'était...

 Lis!
Read the text and answer the questions in English.

1 What did Julie do last Saturday?
2 How many team mates did she have?
3 What did the first group do at midnight?
4 What did the second group do?
5 How did they feel at the finish?

 Écris!
Write about a visit to the cinema, last Saturday (5 sentences).

Example *Samedi dernier, je suis allé(e)... J'ai vu... Ça raconte l'histoire de...*

Une journée dans la vie de... Julie

Samedi dernier, c'était les 24 heures du Mans Rollers. La course a commencé à 16 heures. Julie et ses 10 copains ont participé. À minuit, ils ont continué en deux groupes de cinq rollerskateurs. Le premier groupe a fait quatre heures et le deuxième groupe a dormi. Ensuite, à quatre heures du matin, le premier groupe a dormi et le deuxième a fait quatre heures.

À l'arrivée, ils étaient tous fatigués mais contents. Ils n'ont pas gagné, mais l'ambiance était extraordinaire.

Quel dilemme!

1 Vendredi, 19 h. Louis attend sa petite amie, Anne-Laure, au centre-ville. Sa petite amie? Non, pas encore, mais...?

2 Soudain, Anne-Laure arrive. «Excuse-moi, je suis vraiment désolée, j'ai raté le bus». Puis elle lui prend la main, toute contente: «Viens, on va voir le film?»

3 «On sort demain aussi? J'ai deux billets pour le match France–Italie au Stade de France!»

«Oui, super! Enfin, non... Demain? Euh, je ne sais pas... »

4 «Si tu ne peux pas, j'invite Antonin. Il adore le foot et...»

«Non! Je veux aller au match avec toi, mais...»

«Mais quoi?»

5 «Demain c'est l'anniversaire de ma grand-mère. Elle a 80 ans.»

«Oui, et alors?»

«Et toute la famille va chez elle demain mais je préfère aller au match avec toi!»

 1 **Find the French for these expressions:**

a his girlfriend   d really sorry   g at her house

b not yet   e I missed

c suddenly   f if you can't

2 **Match these titles to paragraphs 1–5.**

a Anne-Laure invites her boyfriend to the match.

b Louis explains the problem to Anne-Laure.

c Anne-Laure apologizes.

d Anne-Laure is dissappointed.

e Louis is waiting for Anne-Laure.

clic-mag

La télé? C'est pour les adultes!

Mon père me dit: «Axel, ne regarde pas la télé réalité, ce n'est pas intéressant.»
Ma mère me demande: «Tu regardes toujours les dessins animés? Ce n'est pas pour toi, c'est pour les petits. »

«Oh non, Axel, encore une émission musicale? Mais c'est nul, le rap. Je déteste ça! Tu es impossible, va au cinéma, va faire du sport!»

Pas de problème, j'adore le sport. ET OUI! Je sais, la télé, c'est bête. Les jeux, les feuilletons, je déteste.

Je ne dis pas à mes parents: «Papa, maman, ne regardez pas la télé réalité, c'est ennuyeux!» Mais ils regardent les émissions de Loft Story* tout le temps! Ils regardent aussi les séries, les téléfilms et les feuilletons. Ils adorent ça!

*Loft Story – a reality-TV show like 'Big Brother'

Moi, je préfère mes jeux de console et l'Internet. Mais mon père me dit: «Axel, tu passes trop de temps avec tes jeux vidéo, c'est nul, ça!»
Mes jeux vidéo maintenant?! Ah, les parents! Qu'est-ce qu'ils m'énervent!

1a **How was Axel feeling when he wrote his blog?**

    a happy   **b** sad   **c** annoyed

1b **How do you know? Explain to your partner (in English).**

2 **Match the French and English phrases:**

    a C'est ennuyeux.   **1** It's for little kids.
    b Ce n'est pas pour toi.   **2** It's stupid.
    c C'est pour les petits.   **3** It's rubbish!
    d Je déteste ça!   **4** Don't watch reality TV.
    e C'est nul!   **5** It's boring.
    f C'est bête.   **6** I prefer the Internet.
    g Je préfère l'internet.   **7** It's not for you.
    h Ne regardez pas la télé réalité.   **8** I hate it!

3 **Pairwork: begin a sentence – can your partner complete it?**

    Example **A** *Le père d'Axel dit: Axel, ne regarde pas la télé réalité, ce n'est pas...?*
              B *...intéressant?*
              A *Oui!*

Vocabulaire

La télévision / *Television*

un dessin animé	*cartoon*
un documentaire	*documentary*
une émission de télé réalité	*reality TV*
une émission musicale	*music programme*
une émission sportive	*sports programme*
un film	*un film*
un feuilleton	*soap (opera)*
les informations	*news*
un jeu télévisé	*TV gameshow*
marrant	*funny*
génial	*great*
bête	*stupid*
ennuyeux / ennuyeuse	*boring*
J'adore...	*I love...*
J'aime bien...	*I like...*
Je déteste les feuilletons / la télé réalité!	*I hate soaps / reality TV!*
J'ai horreur de / des...	*I hate...*
Je n'aime pas (du tout)	*I don't like at all*
très	*very*
assez	*quite*
trop	*too*
Mon émission préférée, c'est...	*My favourite programme is...*

Au grand écran / *On the big screen*

une comédie	*comedy*
un film d'action	*action film*
un film d'amour	*romantic film / love story*
un film de guerre	*war film*
un film d'horreur	*horror film*
un film de science-fiction	*science-fiction film*
l'histoire	*the story*

les effets spéciaux	*special effects*
beau / belle	*handsome / beautiful*
grand / grande	*tall*
naturel / naturelle	*natural*
amusant / amusante	*funny*
intelligent / intelligente	*intelligent*
talentueux / talentueuse	*talented*
mince	*slim*
drôle	*funny*
romantique	*romantic*
sympa	*nice*
Quel genre de film?	*What sort of film?*
J'ai beaucoup aimé...	*I liked a lot...*
Je n'ai pas beaucoup aimé...	*I didn't like a lot...*
c'était	*it was*
C'est un film à voir.	*It's a must see film.*
C'est un film à éviter.	*It's a film to avoid.*
Les effets spéciaux étaient géniaux / nuls.	*The special effects were brilliant / useless*
Mon acteur (actrice) préféré(e)	*My favourite actor*
Mon film préféré	*My favourite film*

Le sport en rêve / *Dream sports*

en automne	*in (the) autumn*
en hiver	*in (the) winter*
en été	*in (the) summer*
au printemps	*in (the) spring*
J'ai participé	*I took part*
Je n'ai pas gagné	*I didn't win*
J'ai fini en deuxième / troisième / dernière position.	*I finished in 2nd / 3rd / last place.*
J'étais...	*I was...*
Tu étais...	*you were...*
arbitre	*referee / umpire*

entraîneur / entraîneuse	*coach / trainer*
joueur / joueuse	*player*
spectateur / spectatrice	*spectator*
fanatique de snowboard	*mad about snowboarding*
extraordinaire comme sport	*an amazing sport*
le championnat	*championship*
l'année dernière	*last year*

WRITING

1 Make up as many sentences as you can about the pictures using the words / phrases on this page.

Pourquoi apprendre le français?

Pour visiter un pays francophone

Où est Monsieur Bean?

Il voyage comment?

Voir page 46.

Des vacances en France?

Où dormir?

Voir pages 48–49.

Le Stade de France: c'est où? C'est quoi?

Le Centre Pompidou: qu'est-ce que c'est?

Voir page 50.

Cyrielle, 19 ans, stagiaire dans un office du tourisme

Elle parle quelles langues?
Pourquoi est-ce utile?

Voir page 52.

Lire en français, tu trouves ça difficile?

Des trucs utiles

Voir page 56.

Qui est-il?
Où habite-t-il?

Pourquoi est-il en danger?

Voir page 59.

À la fin de l'unité 3, reviens ici et réponds aux questions!

On y va?

● Choosing how to travel

Monsieur Bean va en France, mais son voyage n'est pas facile.

READING

1 **Relie les phrases aux photos.**

Exemple *1c,...*

a Il prend le vélo.
b Il prend la mobylette.
c Il prend le train.
d Il est à pied.
e Il prend la voiture.

2 **Quel moyen de transport est le plus populaire? Recopie la liste a–h, écoute et note.**

a *l'avion* ✓✓
b *le bateau* ✓ , etc.

3 **Réécoute et note les adjectifs.**

Exemple *la voiture: rapide, confortable,...*

confortable fatigant long rapide
pratique cher écolo(gique)

Les moyens de transport

l'avion

le bateau

le car

la mobylette

le taxi

le train

la voiture

le vélo

Visit Clic! OxBox

4a **Lis et écoute la conversation. Choisis un titre.**

a Malika et ses copains partent en avion.
b Quatre amis organisent un week-end en Angleterre.

Malika:	Et ce week–end à Oxford? On y* va en bateau?
Simon:	Ah non, le bateau, c'est long. L'avion, c'est mieux*.
	C'est plus rapide que le bateau, et c'est plus confortable.
Malika:	C'est plus cher que le bateau aussi!
Nico:	L'avion n'est pas très écolo – ça pollue l'environnement.
Clara:	Moi, je veux prendre le train. On peut prendre l'Eurostar –
	ça passe par le tunnel sous la Manche. C'est cool.
Simon:	D'accord, le train, c'est moins fatigant que le bateau.
Clara:	Le train, c'est rapide… et c'est moins cher que l'avion.
Nico:	Alors, c'est décidé? On y va en train!

*y = there
mieux = better

 4b **Note les avantages et les inconvénients des transports mentionnés.**

Exemple *le bateau:* *long, etc.*

 4c **Grammaire: trouve les comparatifs dans le texte.**

Exemple *plus rapide = quicker.*

 4d **À quatre: jouez la conversation.**

5 **À deux: comparez.**

Exemple *avion v train*

A *Je préfère prendre l'avion parce que c'est plus rapide.*
B *Mais l'avion est plus cher, et c'est moins écolo.*

a le bus *v* le taxi
b la voiture *v* le vélo
c la mobylette *v* le car

 6 **Choisis six moyens de transport. Tu aimes ou pas? Écris une explication.**

Exemple *Le vélo: J'aime beaucoup le vélo parce que c'est écolo et c'est moins cher.*

Grammaire

Comparing *(le comparatif)*

In French, use **plus** (more) **or moins** (less) before the adjective to compare two things:

c'est plus (+) / moins (–) → cher / confortable / long / écolo / fatigant / rapide

L'avion est plus rapide.
The plane is quicker.

plus / moins … que = more / less … than
Le bateau est moins cher que l'avion.
The boat is less expensive than the plane.

Où dormir?

● Choosing holiday accommodation

Jeu-test: Les meilleures vacances pour toi

1 La destination la plus intéressante?
a la plage
b la montagne
c le centre de vacances

2 L'hébergement que tu préfères?
a un hôtel cinq étoiles
b un camping sympa
c une auberge de jeunesse*   *youth hostel

3 Les activités les plus amusantes?
a bronzer
b faire des excursions
c faire du sport

4 Les compagnons les plus sympa?
a la famille
b les copains
c les nouveaux amis qu'on se fait

1 Lis le jeu-test et trouve les expressions pour dire:

a the best holiday   c sunbathing
b the beach   d the new friends you make

2 L'illustration avec chaque question va avec la réponse a, b ou c?

Exemple *1a,...*

3 **Grammaire:** recopie les questions du jeu-test et donne l'équivalent en anglais.

Exemple *La destination la plus intéressante* = The most interesting destination

4 Fais le jeu-test. Lis l'analyse. C'est vrai pour toi?

Analyse

Une majorité de a: Pour toi, le plus important, c'est le confort.

Une majorité de b: Pour toi, le plus important, c'est l'aventure.

Une majorité de c: Tu es très sociable. Le plus important, c'est de t'amuser avec les autres.

le / la / les plus = the most

le / la / les moins = the least

la fille la plus belle
the most beautiful girl

le musée le plus intéressant
the most interesting museum

les activités les plus intéressantes
the most interesting activities

Visit **Clic!** ⌐ReBox

5a Écoute et note les types d'hébergement dans l'ordre.

Exemple *c,...*

 5b Réécoute. Prends des notes en français.
a Where did they stay?
b How was it?

Exemple *1   a hôtel, b confortable / un peu snob.*

 5c Réponds aux questions pour chaque jeune. Utilise tes notes.

A Tu es allé(e) où?
B Je suis allé(e) dans un hôtel.
A C'était comment?
B C'était très confortable.

6a Lis les bulles. Résume les vacances de Romain et de Malika en 1–2 phrases.

> L'année dernière, j'ai fait du camping en Espagne. C'était génial. La plus grande attraction pour moi, c'était la vie en plein air. Mais une tente n'a pas de salle de bains. On va au bloc sanitaire pour se brosser les dents.

Malika

> En Irlande, je suis resté dans une auberge de jeunesse. Ce n'est pas le grand luxe mais c'est la solution la moins chère. C'était sympa.

Romain

 6b À deux: décrivez un voyage (réel ou imaginaire). Utilise les bulles de l'activité 6a comme modèle.

– *Tu es allé(e) où?*
– *Tu es resté(e) où?*
– *C'était comment?*

L'hébergement

a *j'ai fait du camping*

b *je suis parti(e) en caravane*

c *je suis allé(e) dans un hôtel*

d *j'ai loué un gîte*

e *je suis allé(e) dans une auberge de jeunesse (une AJ)*

Stratégies

Make your writing more interesting!

- Use words like *très, un peu, beaucoup* before adjectives.
  C'était très confortable. It was very comfortable.

- Add a couple of details, for example which town / country you went to, whether you were at the seaside etc.
  Je suis allé(e) en France au bord de la mer.

- Say what your favourite activity was:
  Mon activitée préférée, c'était le surf.

L'année derniére	j'ai	fait du camping		
		loué une caravane / un gîte		
	je suis	allé(e)	dans	un hôtel / une auberge de jeunesse.
		resté(e)		
		parti(e) en caravane.		
C'était	snob			
Ce n'était pas	super			
	confortable			
	cher			
	genial			
	sympa			
	nul pratique			

En balade à Paris

● Visiting Paris

1 Lis les annonces. Comment dit-on...?

a go up to the top of the tower
b from the third floor
c open from 9 am until midnight
d closed on Tuesdays
e how to get there
f full price/reduced price

2 Réponds en anglais aux questions des touristes.

a Our hotel is in the south of Paris. Is the Eiffel Tower near there?

b What's the nearest metro station to the Eiffel Tower?

c What can you do at the Georges Pompidou Centre?

d Is the centre open in the mornings?

e Is the *Cité des Sciences* closed on a Sunday?

f How much will it cost for one adult and one child to see an IMAX film?

La tour Eiffel

Montez au sommet de la tour. Du troisième étage, admirez Paris. **Ouverture** de 9 h à minuit (mai-juin – fin août) **Prix**: adulte: 11,50 euros, enfant: 6,30 euros
Comment y aller: Située sur le Champ de Mars, dans l'ouest de Paris.
Métro: station Champ de Mars–Tour Eiffel

Le Centre Georges Pompidou

Admirez l'architecture moderne, visitez le Musée National d'Art Moderne, et allez voir une exposition, un film ou un concert.
Ouverture tous les jours de 11 h à 21 h.
Fermé le mardi.
Prix: 10 euros
Comment y aller: Situé place Beaubourg, dans le centre de Paris.
Métro: station Rambuteau

La Cité des Sciences et de l'Industrie

Découvrez les sciences, visitez le planétarium, regardez un film IMAX à la Géode. Ouvert de 10 h à 18 h (dimanche à 19 h).
Fermé le lundi.
Prix: (pour un film IMAX) 9 euros plein tarif, 7 euros tarif réduit
Comment y aller:
Située à La Villette, dans le nord-est de Paris.
Métro: station Porte de la Villette

Visit

À deux: décidez:

a the most expensive activity for an adult.
b the cheapest place / activity for a child.
c the place with the longest opening hours.
d the most interesting place / activity.

 Écoute et lis. Relie la conversation à une des photos de la page 50.

Vous pouvez me recommander une visite?
Vous pouvez visiter <u>la tour Eiffel</u>.

C'est où?
C'est <u>dans l'ouest de Paris</u>.

Quelle est la station de métro la plus proche?
Il y a la station de métro <u>Champ de Mars−Tour Eiffel</u>.

Ça ouvre à quelle heure?
C'est ouvert de <u>9 heures</u> à <u>minuit</u>.

Ça coûte combien?
C'est <u>11,50 euros pour un adulte et 6,30 euros pour un enfant si on monte au sommet</u>.

Qu'est-ce qu'on y fait?
Vous pouvez <u>monter au sommet de la tour pour avoir une belle vue sur Paris</u>.

Stratégies

Rappel: *Les questions*

1 Use intonation − make your voice go up at the end:
Vous pouvez me recommander une visite?
(you can add **est-ce que** to the start of a sentence as an alternative: *Est-ce que vous pouvez me recommander une visite?*)

2 Use a question word:
Où? = Where?
Quel / Quelle? = What / Which?
Combien? = How much / many?
Qu'est-ce que? = What?

 À deux: jouez le dialogue.

 Adaptez le dialogue aux deux annonces qui restent. Changez les mots soulignés.

Exemple **A** *Vous pouvez me recommander une visite?*
B *Vous pouvez visiter le Centre Georges Pompidou, etc.*

 Écrivez le dialogue pour le Centre Pompidou ou la Cité des Sciences.

C'est la vie!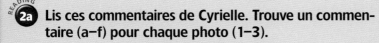

VIDEO

1 Avant de regarder le clip, choisis trois endroits que tu vas peut-être voir. Ensuite, regarde le clip pour vérifier.

a inside a tourist office   **d** a harbour
b a church   **e** a park
c an island   **f** a fish market

READING

2a Lis ces commentaires de Cyrielle. Trouve un commentaire (a–f) pour chaque photo (1–3).

a «J'aime beaucoup renseigner les visiteurs.»
b «Je trouve mon travail assez agréable.»
c «Ranger les brochures, c'est ennuyeux.»
d «Le pire, c'est de faire les photocopies.»
e «Je réponds aux emails − c'est intéressant.»
f «C'est la plus belle ville du monde.»

READING

2b Les commentaires sont positifs ou négatifs?

Cyrielle, 19 ans, stagiaire à l'office du tourisme de Marseille

Pour ceux qui veulent savoir

Des visites commentées, à pied ou en car de 5 à 14 €
Le stade Vélodrome, le Panier "plus vieux quartier de Marseille", l'Estaque et ses peintres, Notre Dame de la Garde, sur les pas de Marcel Pagnol.

VIDEO

3 **Regarde le clip et note en français:**

a The tourists' nationalities
b Cyrielle's favourite language
c The best way to visit Marseille: by foot, bus or train?

> On the badge that Cyrielle wears to work are some little flags. What do you think they are for?

WRITING

4a **Recopie les questions a–f. Souligne les mots interrogatifs. Ensuite, traduis les questions en anglais.**

WRITING

4b **Réponds aux questions pour Cyrielle.**

Exemple *Je travaille à l'office du tourisme de Marseille. Etc.*

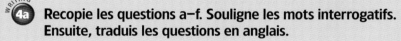
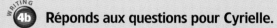

a Tu travailles où? *Je travaille...*
b Comment trouves-tu le travail?
 Je trouve mon travail...
c Qu'est-ce que tu fais exactement à l'office du tourisme? *Je fais...Je...*
d Qui sont les touristes? *Les touristes sont...*
e Tu parles quelles langues? *Je...*
f Quelle est la plus belle attraction de la ville? *La plus belle... , c'est...*

Grammaire

Question words

Qu'est-ce que... + verb***?*** = What...?

Qui? = Who?

Comment? = How?

Pourquoi? = Why?

Où? = Where?

Quel (Quelle / Quels / Quelles)... + noun***?*** = What / Which...?

Quand? = Why?

Combien? = How much? / How many?

Le sais-tu?
● Marseille is a multi-cultural city, the second largest in France, after Paris.
● It is by the Mediterranean sea and is the largest commercial port in France.
● Films shot partly in Marseille: *The French Connection, The Bourne Identity, Love Actually, The Devil Wears Prada.*

SPEAKING

5 **À deux: jouez l'interview avec les questions a–f.**

WRITING

6 **Écris un paragraphe.**
Imagine you are doing work experience in a tourist office in your town. In French, answer all the questions in activity 4.

Exemple *Je travaille à l'office du tourisme de Bradford...*, etc.

Labo-langue

Verb + infinitive

Q: What is an infinitive?

A: The form of the verb that ends *–er, -ir* or *–re* is the **infinitive**. This is the form you find in a dictionary.

 A ***aller* + infinitive**
To talk about the near future, something that will almost certainly happen, use: ***aller* + infinitive**

Je vais venir. (= I am going to come.)
Tu vas venir. (= You are going to come.)
Il/Elle/On va venir. (= He/She/It is going to come.)

Nous allons venir. (= We are going to come.)
Vous allez venir. (= You are going to come.)
Ils/Elles vont venir. (= They are going to come.)

Demain, je vais prendre le train.

1a **Copy these sentences, filling each gap with the correct form of *aller*.**

a   Je ✳✳✳ organiser des vacances en France.
b   Tu ✳✳✳ prendre l'avion?
c   Il ✳✳✳ venir chez nous demain soir.
d   Tu ✳✳✳ rester dans une auberge de jeunesse?
e   Le film ✳✳✳ commencer dans cinq minutes.
f   On ✳✳✳ trouver un camping au bord de la mer.

1b **Translate sentences a–f into English.**

2 **Translate these sentences into French, using *aller* + infinitive.**

a   The train is going to leave.
b   Are you going to come to the cinema with us?
c   I'm not going to go to the station.
d   My parents are going to arrive in ten minutes.
e   We are going to visit the *Stade de France* tomorrow.
f   My grandmother is going to live in England.

 B ***il faut* + infinitive**
il faut (which means 'you have to'*)
or
il ne faut pas ('you don't have to' or 'you mustn't') } + infinitive

Il faut rentrer avant minuit.
= You have to be back before midnight.
Il ne faut pas oublier les billets.
= You mustn't forget the tickets.

3 **Copy the sentences, choosing an infinitive from the box to fill the gaps.**

a   Il faut ✳✳✳ le train à la gare.
b   Il faut ✳✳✳ français le plus souvent possible.
c   Il faut ✳✳✳ du sport.
d   Il ne faut pas ✳✳✳ ton passeport.
e   Il ne faut pas ✳✳✳ timide.

faire   être   parler   prendre   oublier

4 **Put the words in the right order to make sentences.**

a   en France aller il faut
b   il prendre taxi faut un
c   faut téléphoner mes il à parents
d   ne pas il faut sortir
e   il faut réserver l'avance ne pas à

Visit

C *aimer, vouloir, pouvoir* + infinitive

J'aime sortir. = I like going out.
Je veux sortir. = I want to go out.
Je peux sortir. = I can go out.

Je n'aime pas sortir. = I don't like going out.
Je ne veux pas sortir. = I don't want to go out.
Je ne peux pas sortir. = I can't go out.

See the full pattern of the present tense of these verbs on pages 144–145.

Tu ne veux pas faire comme moi?

5 Look back over pages 46–51. How many examples of verb + infinitive can you find and list in three minutes?

6a Copy the sentences, choosing the right verb.

a J'aime **pars** / **partir** en vacances.
b Tu veux **aller** / **vas** à Paris?
c Il **peut** / **pouvoir** prendre le train.
d On ne **veut** / **vouloir** pas visiter les monuments.
e Je **peux** / **pouvoir** **mange** / **manger** au restaurant.
f Tu **vouloir** / **veux** **visiter** / **visite** le camping?

6b Translate sentences a–f into English.

D *pour* + infinitive

When *pour* means 'in order to' and is followed by a verb, that verb is always in the infinitive.

J'ai téléphoné pour réserver une chambre.
= I phoned (in order) to reserve a room.

Marc joue de la guitare pour gagner de l'argent.

7 Read Malika's text on page 49. Note the examples of *pour* + infinitive and give the English equivalents.

8 Choose endings for these sentences.

a On va aller en France pour...
b Il faut acheter un billet pour...
c Je veux prendre un taxi pour...
d Nous allons à l'office du tourisme pour...
e Léo est sorti pour...
f Je vais au collège pour...
g On peut prendre le bus pour...
h Ils vont à l'aéroport pour...

Reading French texts takes so long when you have to look up every word.

When I read, I always look for key words, like we're told, but sometimes it doesn't help.

Good news! You don't have to look up every word. In a long passage, it is most likely there will be a number of new words or phrases you will be able to work out.

- Before you start reading, make use of any clues: layout, pictures, title, introduction. Sometimes it helps to read through the questions or tasks first.
- Read the text through quite quickly at first, to try to get the gist. Skim over any words you don't understand.
- Make sensible guesses. If a word starts with a capital letter, it is probably the name of a person or a place.
- Is the word similar to an English word or another French word you know?

It is always a good idea to identify which are the key words in a text and what they mean.

However, your job does not stop there. Don't make the mistake of ignoring the little words. Here are some that can alter meaning.

> *ou* (**or**)
> *et* (**and**)
> *sans* (**without**)
> *sauf* (**except**)
> *plus* (**more**)
> *moins* (**less**)
> *avant* (**before**)
> *après* (**after**)

READING

3 The key word(s) alone will not help you understand these sentences. Identify the little words that are important and answer the questions in English.

a Mon père est arrivé après minuit.

Do we know the precise time he arrived?

b Il faut un passeport et un visa pour aller aux USA.

Do you need both or just one?

c Je prends des euros ou des chèques de voyage?

Does the speaker think both are necessary?

d Le car est parti sans nous.

Did they go in the coach?

e J'aime tous les sports, sauf le tennis.

Does the speaker like tennis?

READING

1 Work out the meaning of the underlined words. (Use a dictionary to check afterwards.) Which of the tips above did you use?

a Le président est arrivé <u>en hélicoptère</u>.
b Il y avait <u>des volcans</u> en France.
c Je cherche <u>le guichet</u> où on peut acheter les billets.
d On peut acheter un ticket de métro ou <u>un carnet</u> de dix tickets (c'est moins cher).
e Il y a trop de <u>publicités</u> entre les émissions à la télé.

SPEAKING

3 Turn to page 59. Use the advice above. Discuss with a partner if any of the tips were helpful.

Écoute!

1a Listen and select two letters for each speaker.

Example 1 b/C

1
a  b  c
A rapide
B long
C confortable

2
a  b c
A fatigant
B intéressant
C écolo

3
a  b c
A rapide
B confortable
C long

4
a  b c
A cher
B rapide
C long

5
a  b c
A fatigant
B écolo
C cher

6
a b c
A intéressant
B confortable
C rapide

Parle!

3 Look at the pictures and say where you went on holiday last year and how you got there.

Example Je suis allé(e) en Irlande. Je suis allé(e) dans un hôtel.

Lis!

2 Read the message and answer the questions.

a Where did Valentin stay when he went to the mountains?
b What was good about this year's holiday?
c What was not so good about it?
d Where did he go on holiday last year?
e Who did he go with?
f What did he like best at the campsite?
g Does he prefer camping or hotels?
h Where is he going to stay when he goes to Paris?
i Who is he going to go with?
j What are they going to do in Paris?

Cette année, je suis allé dans un hôtel à la montagne. C'était très confortable, mais c'était un peu ennuyeux.

L'année dernière, c'était plus intéressant. Avec ma famille, on a fait du camping à la campagne.

Le camping, c'est plus amusant. L'attraction la plus intéressante pour moi, c'était la piscine.

Pour moi, la destination la plus intéressante, c'est Paris. Le week-end prochain, je vais aller dans une auberge de jeunesse à Paris avec mes deux frères. On va visiter tous les monuments, mais pour moi, la visite la plus importante, c'est Disneyland.

Valentin, 15 ans

Écris!

4 Invent a visit to France. Write 50+ words.

Example Je suis allé(e) + place. Je suis resté(e) + accomodation etc.

a where you went?
c what means of transport you used
d where you stayed
b how you travelled
e what you thought of it

Quel dilemme!

1

«Tu vas où, Carine?», demande le père de Carine. Elle dit qu'elle va en ville, chez une copine.
«Tu rentres à dix heures, OK? Sinon, attention à toi!»
«Oui, Papa. Pas de problème.»
Carine est contente de quitter la maison. Il fait beau. Elle va chez Nadia à pied.

2

Carine s'amuse beaucoup chez Nadia. Elles regardent un peu la télé. C'est la Star Ac' – son émission préférée. La mère de Nadia est très cool!
À 21 heures 40, Carine dit au revoir. Vite, elle va prendre son bus pour ne pas rentrer en retard*.

*late

3

Carine arrive à l'arrêt de bus. Le bus est en retard.
Elle regarde dans son sac. Où est son porte-monnaie? Ah non, il est dans sa chambre, sur son lit! Catastrophe! Elle n'a pas d'argent pour le ticket de bus.

4

Carine tremble. Son père va être furieux. Qu'est-ce qu'elle va faire?
Soudain, elle voit une enveloppe par terre avec un nom et une adresse: Julie Meunier, 4, place Jamin. Elle l'ouvre. Il y a 50 euros dans l'enveloppe.
Un taxi passe. Carine regarde le taxi et l'argent. En taxi, elle peut rentrer à la maison avant dix heures. Mais ce n'est pas son argent.

Carine hésite. Qu'est-ce qu'elle va faire?

1 **Without using a dictionary, work out the English for the words that are underlined. (See strategies on page 56.)**

Example *émission* = programme

2 **Read the story and answer the questions.**
a Where is Carine going?
b What time does she have to be home?
c What does she do at Nadia's?
d What time does she leave Nadia's house?
e What can't she find in her bag?
f Where does she find some money?
g What is she tempted to do with the money?

3 **Which of the following do you think is the most likely ending to the story?**

A Carine prend un taxi et arrive à la maison à dix heures.

B Carine met l'enveloppe avec l'argent dans son sac. Demain, elle va aller place Jamin et rendre* l'argent. Elle rentre à pied.

*give back

C Carine ne prend pas l'argent pour elle. Elle téléphone à son père. Il va peut-être comprendre.

D Le bus arrive. Carine prend 10 euros pour acheter un ticket de bus. À la maison, elle va remplacer les 10 euros. Et demain, elle va donner l'enveloppe à la police.

Visit clic! OxBox

clic-mag

Les gorilles menacés d'extinction

Un grand **nombre** d'animaux en Afrique – le gorille, le lion, l'éléphant, le chimpanzé – sont en danger.

Le Parc des Virunga est un **parc protégé**, en Afrique. **Le gorille** de montagne habite dans le Parc des Virunga.

Le gorille des montagnes, est un peu différent des autres gorilles. Il a le **poil** plus long et plus **sombre**. Il a de grandes mâchoires et un plus petit museau. Il mange des feuilles, mais aussi des fleurs, des fruits, des champignons et quelquefois des insectes!

Le gorille est notre cousin. Il est très intelligent. Mais on **chasse** les gorilles et on les tue. En plus, beaucoup de gorilles sont tués pendant **les guerres civiles**. Avec tous ces dangers, les gorilles de montagne vont bientôt **disparaître**.

C'est le logo de la WWF. Consultez son site web pour plus d'informations.

Before reading this article, look back over the tips in Forum on page 56.

READING
1 Read the article quickly. Which statement is right: a or b?

a The article is about safari holidays in Africa.
b The article is about endangered species in Africa.

READING
2 Without looking in a dictionary, work out the English for the words in bold type.

SPEAKING
3 You can look up no more than three words in the dictionary. Discuss with a partner which words you chose and why.

WRITING
4 Summarise the article in English (approx. **100** words).

3.8 Vocabulaire

Les moyens de transport	Means of transport
Tu voyages comment?	How do you travel?
Je prends...	I travel by...
l'avion	plane
le bateau	boat
le car	coach
la mobylette	moped
le taxi	taxi
le train	train
le vélo	bike
la voiture	car
c'est rapide	it's fast
cher	expensive
confortable	comfortable
écolo	environmentally friendly
fatigant	tiring
long	long

Comparer	Comparing
plus... (que...)	more.... (than...)
moins... (que...)	less... (than...)
L'avion est plus cher (que le bateau).	The plane is more expensive (than the boat).
La voiture est moins fatigante (que le train).	The car is less tiring (than the train).
la destination la plus intéressante	the most interesting destination

L'hébergement	Accommodation
J'ai fait du camping.	I went camping.
Je suis parti(e) en caravane	I went caravanning
Je suis allé(e) dans un hôtel	I went to a hotel
Je suis allé(e) dans une auberge de jeunesse	I went to a youth hostel
J'ai loué un gîte	I rented a cottage / gite
Je suis allé(e) dans un hôtel au bord de la mer.	I went to a hotel at the seaside.
On a fait du camping à la campagne.	We went camping in the country.

C'était confortable	It was comfortable.
cher	expensive
sympa	nice / friendly
génial	great
pratique	practical
snob	posh

Les visites	Sightseeing
Vous pouvez me recommander une visite?	Can you recommend a place to visit?
Vous pouvez visiter la tour Eiffel.	You can visit the Eiffel Tower.
C'est où?	Where is it?
C'est dans l'ouest de Paris.	It's in the west of Paris.
Quelle est la station de métro la plus proche?	What is the nearest metro station?
Ça ouvre à quelle heure?	What time does it open?
C'est ouvert de 9 heures à minuit.	It's open from 9 am until midnight.
ouvert tous les jours/de 9 h à 12 h/de juin à août	open every day/from 9 to 12/from June to August
fermé le mardi	closed on Tuesdays
Ça coûte combien?	How much does it cost?
C'est 11,50 euros pour un adulte / un enfant.	It's 11 euros 50 for an adult / a child.
Qu'est-ce qu'on y fait?	What is there to do there?
Vous pouvez (monter en haut de la tour).	You can (go up the tower).
Je vais aller (au Stade de France).	I'm going to go (to the Stade de France).
On va faire une visite guidée.	We're going to have a guided tour.
Je vais voir une exposition.	I'm going to see an exhibition.

Les questions	Question words
où?	where?
qui?	who?
quand?	when?
pourquoi?	why?
quel / quelle?	what / which?
combien?	how much / how many?
qu'est-ce que?	what?

 WRITING

1 Make up as many sentences as you can about the pictures using the words / phrases on this page.

Pourquoi apprendre le français?

Pour les vacances ou le travail en France

Les repas en France

C'est quoi, tes repas préférés?
Tu es végétarien(ne)?

Voir page 64.

Comment aider pendant un séjour?

Et chez toi, tu aides souvent?

Voir page 66.

Qui est déjà allé en France?

C'était comment?

Voir page 68.

Savoir-vivre 4

C'est comment, la vie dans une famille à l'étranger?

Tu voudrais être au pair?

Voir page 70.

Que faire si tu ne connais pas un mot?

On ne te comprend pas?

Qu'est-ce que tu peux faire?

Voir page 74.

La petite amie de son correspondant veut sortir avec Tom.

Qu'est-ce qu'il doit faire?

À toi de décider!

Voir page 76.

À la fin de l'unité 4, reviens ici et réponds aux questions!

Repas de famille

● Coping at the meal table

 1a Qu'est-ce que Daniel a mangé à midi? Devine et écris cinq choses. Il a bu du coca ou de l'eau minérale?

Exemple *Il a mangé du pain, du fromage... Il a bu...*

Daniel va chez Clément, son correspondant français.

a  du pain

b  du fromage

c  du pâté

d  du coca

e  un yaourt

f de l'eau minérale

g  de la salade

h  une banane

i  des chips

j  des tomates

 1b Écoute et vérifie.

Rappel: *some, any*

le coca	**du** coca
l'eau minérale	**de l'**eau minérale
la salade	**de la** salade
les chips	**des** chips

Ballade de la salade

La soupe de poisson, les fruits de mer,
La truite, le saumon, les moules marinière.
J'adore tout ça, c'est fantastique,
Mais tu **ne** manges **rien**?
Tu es allergique?

Non, je **ne** mange **plus**
de poisson, c'est bien vrai,
Je déteste le steak, le porc et le poulet.
Je **ne** mange **jamais** de viande,
mais ça **ne** me rend **pas** malade...

...D'accord, alors mange de la salade!

Grammaire

Using negatives

ne (or **n'**) goes before the verb and **pas / plus / jamais / rien** goes after the verb. After negatives, **du**, **de l'**, **de la** and **des** become **de**.

Je mange de la pizza.	I eat pizza.
Je **ne** mange **pas de** pizza.	I don't eat pizza.
Je **ne** mange **plus de** pizza.	I don't eat pizza any more.
Je **ne** mange **jamais de** pizza.	I never eat pizza.
Je **ne** mange **rien**.	I eat nothing.

2 Écoute et lis.

3 À deux: **A** dit une phrase et **B** dit le contraire.

Exemple **A** *Je mange du poisson. J'aime ça!*
B *Je ne mange pas de poisson. Je n'aime pas ça!*

Visit Clic! OxBox

4a Écoute la conversation à table.

 4b À deux: vous êtes à table. A pose les questions 1-7 et B répond aux questions.

1 Tu aimes la salade de tomates?
2 Sers-toi, alors.
3 Tu peux me passer le poivre?
4 Du pain?
5 On mange de la pizza. Tu aimes ça?
6 Tu veux encore de la pizza?
7 Et comme dessert, il y a de la crème caramel. Tu aimes ça?

Merci, monsieur / madame.
Oui, je veux bien. Merci, monsieur / madame.
Oui, j'adore ça. C'est délicieux.
Non merci, madame / monsieur, mais c'était délicieux.
Oui, bien sûr. Voilà.
Oui, j'aime beaucoup. C'est bon.
Oui, merci, c'est mon dessert préféré.

Grammaire

Rappel

Remember to use **vous** when you talk to your friend's / penpal's parents, even if they call you **tu**:

*Vous **pouvez** me passer la pizza, s'il **vous** plaît, <u>monsieur</u>?*

*Tu **peux** me passer l'eau, s'il **te** plaît, <u>Clément</u>?*

 5 Tu es comment à table? Choisis tes réponses honnêtement!

Fais le test-politesse! Tu réponds comment?

Tu es très poli(e), assez poli(e) ou impoli(e) à table?

1 **Tu veux de la salade de concombre?**
  a Beurk! Je déteste ça!
  b Oui, je veux bien, merci.
  c Ah non, je ne mange jamais de salade.

2 **Tu aimes les lasagnes?**
  a Non, j'ai assez mangé.
  b Oui, c'est très bon.
  c Non, sers-toi.

3 **Tu peux me passer l'eau, s'il te plaît?**
  a Bien sûr, voilà.
  b Non, merci, je ne veux pas d'eau.
  c Non, sers-toi!

4 **Tu veux encore du steak haché?**
  a Non, je suis végétarien, monsieur.
  b OK.
  c Non, merci, j'ai assez mangé.

5 **Tu me passes du pain, s'il te plaît?**
  a Du quoi?
  b Oh, c'est délicieux.
  c Oui, voilà.

6 **C'était bon, la salade de fruits?**
  a Bof! Pas tellement.
  b Oui, c'était délicieux, merci, madame.
  c Oui, mais je ne mange pas de fruits.

Compte tes points:

	a	b	c
1	a0	b3	c0
2	a0	b3	c0
3	a3	b0	c0
4	a0	b0	c3
5	a0	b0	c3
6	a0	b3	c0

Résultats

15–18 Félicitations! Tu es très poli(e).
11–15 Bien! Tu es assez poli(e).
6–10 Attention, tu n'es pas tellement poli(e)!
0–5 Oh, tu es très impoli(e)!

Qui aide à la maison?

● Helping around the house

a

lundi

b mardi

c

mercredi

d

jeudi

e

vendredi

f

samedi

g dimanche

Je peux / Tu peux...

ranger la chambre
faire la vaisselle
faire la cuisine
passer l'aspirateur
mettre le couvert
débarrasser la table
faire mon / ton lit

 1 **Écoute. C'est quelle image?**

Exemple *1g*

 2 SPEAKING **À deux: A choisit le jour pour aider et B répond.**

Exemple   **A** *(Vendredi). Je peux t'aider?*
        B *Oui, bien sûr. (**v**endredi = **v**aisselle) Tu peux faire la vaisselle.*
        A *D'accord.*

lundi = faire mon **l**it
mardi = ranger **ma** chambre
mercredi = **me**ttre le couvert
vendredi = faire la **v**aisselle
samedi = pa**ss**er l'a**s**pirateur
dimanche = **d**ébarrasser la table

 3 **Écoute et note les détails de Daniel en anglais. Lis *Adverbs of time / frequency*, page 67.**

	task	when?
1	I make the bed	every day
2	I...	

Visit **Clic!** OxBox

W R I T I N G **4** Regarde les images et fais des phrases.

Exemple *a Je fais mon lit tous les jours.*

tous les jours

souvent

de temps en temps

rarement

ne... jamais

Adverbs of time / frequency

Use these to say how often you do things. They usually go after the verb, though *d'habitude* often starts the sentence.

tous les jours = every day
    Je fais la vaisselle *tous les jours.*
d'habitude = usually
    D'habitude, elle passe l'aspirateur.
souvent = often
    Tu débarrasses *souvent* la table?
de temps en temps = from time to time
    Je fais mon lit *de temps en temps.*
rarement = not often, rarely
    Je range *rarement* ma chambre.
ne... jamais = never
    Il *ne* met *jamais* le couvert.

 5a Recopie la grille ci-dessous, écoute et note les points.

 SPEAKING **5b** À deux: faites le quiz 'Champion pour aider à la maison'.

Exemple **B** *Tu fais souvent la cuisine?*
    A *Non, je fais rarement la cuisine. (1 point) Et toi?*
    B *Je fais la cuisine de temps en temps. (2 points), … etc.*

(D'habitude,)	Je	fais range passe débarrasse mets	(souvent) (rarement)	mon lit la cuisine l'aspirateur la table le couvert	(de temps en temps) (tous les jours)
Je	ne	fais range	jamais	la vaisselle. ma chambre.	

QUIZ:

CHAMPION POUR AIDER À LA MAISON

Qui aide le plus à la maison, les garçons ou les filles?

1 Tu fais souvent la cuisine?

2 Tu ranges ta chambre quand?

3 Et la table, tu la débarrasses tous les jours?

4 Tu fais la vaisselle de temps en temps?

5 Tu passes souvent l'aspirateur?

6 Tu mets souvent le couvert?

	Garçons	Filles	Fréquence	Points
1			Tous les jours	5
2			D'habitude	4
3			Souvent	3
4			De temps en temps	2
5			Rarement	1
6			Jamais	0

Vive la différence!

● Discussing lifestyles

 1a Lis le blog. Retrouve les légendes des photos.

Exemple **1c**

a Normalement, le dîner est à vingt heures.

b Le déjeuner au collège dure une heure et demie.

c On peut conduire une mobylette à 14 ans!

d En général, en France, on n'aime pas faire la queue!

e Au petit déjeuner, on boit son café ou chocolat chaud dans un bol.

f Chaque matin, on achète du pain frais.

g En ville, beaucoup de gens habitent dans un appartement.

h Souvent, on a des cartes pour sa fête.

 1b Les photos sont prises en France. Pourquoi? Explique en anglais.

Exemple **2** *Hot chocolate is being drunk from a bowl.*

2a Écoute le podcast de Daniel sur les différences entre la France et la Grande-Bretagne. Quelles parties du podcast (1–8) correspondent aux phrases (a–h) de l'activité 1?

Exemple **1** *a*

2b Réécoute. Il préfère les traditions en France ou en Grande-Bretagne?

Exemple **1** *Grande-Bretagne* 😊

 2c À deux: **A** dit cinq phrases. **B** décide si c'est en France ou en Grande-Bretagne.

Exemple **A** *Le soir, on mange à vingt heures.*
B *C'est en France.*

Stratégies

How to listen to longer texts

- Remember: you are not expected to understand every word!
- Look for clues about what the text is about in the instructions
- Look for clues in the photos 1–4 and texts a–h.
- Listen for key words, e.g. *dîner, déjeuner, chocolat chaud* etc.

Visit **Clic!** OxBox

Pendant son séjour en France, Daniel assiste à une fête familiale: la première communion de Lucille, la cousine de Clément.

 Lis l'histoire et écoute.

1 Le dimanche matin, à 10 heures...

Qu'est-ce que tu fais? C'est horrible!

C'est intéressant! Je n'ai jamais assisté à une communion avant.

2 Pendant la cérémonie religieuse à l'église...

Ben, j'essaie de chanter en français! Tu n'aimes pas?

3 On fait de beaux cadeaux pour la communion.

Oh non! J'ai oublié de faire un cadeau! Je suis désolé!

On t'aide à ouvrir tous tes cadeaux, Lucille?

4 À une heure, on commence à manger.

J'ai déja encouragé Daniel à goûter mais il refuse de manger des fruits de mer!

Tu essaies de manger quelques huîtres*?

*oysters

5 À six heures, on continue de manger.

6 Quoi, on va recommencer à manger? Ah non! Impossible!

Ils n'ont pas encore fini de manger? Moi, je ne peux plus bouger!

Allez! Viens m'aider à débarrasser! Il faut commencer à préparer le repas de ce soir!

Bienvenue en France!

 Écris un résumé de l'histoire en anglais.

 Écoute. C'est quelle photo?

Exemple   **1** = *photo 3*

 À trois: jouez l'histoire. Si vous voulez, changez des détails.

Exemple   *Lucille: Tu essaies de manger quelques **olives**?*
           Daniel: Beurk!
           Clément: J'ai déjà encouragé Daniel à goûter mais il
                      *refuse de manger des **olives**!*

Voici Marie Torresani et Isis Nesta, à Marseille. Marie a passé six semaines dans une famille en Angleterre et Isis a passé six semaines dans une famille en Irlande.

VIDÉO
1a Regarde le clip et observe bien. Lis a–d. Tu es d'accord ou pas?

a Marie is short and she has long dark hair.
b Marseille isn't by the sea.
c Isis likes horses.
d There are many animals on the sofa.

VIDÉO
1b À deux: qu'est-ce que vous avez remarqué dans le clip? Discutez en anglais.

Exemple *The weather in Marseille looks sunny but not hot.*

VIDÉO
2a Lis ces questions posées à Marie et Isis. Mets-les dans l'ordre du clip. Regarde et vérifie.

a Tu as aidé la famille?
c Tu as rencontré des jeunes Anglais?
b Tu voudrais repartir?
d Qu'est-ce qui t'a étonnée?

VIDÉO
2b Complète les réponses de Marie ou Isis avec les mots de la boîte. Regarde encore le clip et vérifie.

a J'ai [1] des jeunes Anglais sur la plage.
b Oui, j'ai [2] avec la [3] dans le centre équestre*. *horse–riding centre
c Ce qui m'a [4] là–bas, ce sont les associations de nourriture puisque j'ai mangé des pâtes à la [5] avec des frites.
d Oui, j'aimerais [6] repartir parce que ça m'a vraiment beaucoup [7].

beaucoup	bolognaise	étonnée
famille	plu	rencontré
travaillé		

VIDÉO
3 Regarde encore. Indique quand tu entends ces mots. C'est quoi en anglais?

a un nouveau pays
b une nouvelle culture
c perfectionner notre anglais
d connaître de nouvelles personnes
e voyager un peu plus
f parler anglais toute la journée

4 **À deux: regardez les photos. A choisit la bonne phrase 1-4 et B dit quelle photo c'est.**

Exemple **A** *J'ai rencontré des jeunes Anglais.*
B *C'est la photo a.*

1 J'ai rencontré des jeunes anglais.
2 J'ai passé six semaines avec une famille anglaise.
3 J'ai travaillé dans un centre équestre.
4 On a fêté l'anniversaire de la fille.

5 **On parle du travail au pair en France. C'est positif ou négatif? Fais deux listes.**

Le sais-tu?

- The kites, flags and windmills on the beach are part of the *Fête du vent*. There are kite festivals (*Festivals du cerf-volant*) all over France.
- The first *Fête du vent* in Marseille was in 1987. Since then it has become a major five-day event, with kite-flying demonstrations, exhibitions and workshops for children and the disabled.
- If you're aged 18–27, you can work as an au pair. This usually means spending a year abroad working for a family. You improve your language skills and get paid for it!

a J'aime travailler avec les enfants, heureusement.

b J'ai perfectionné mon français et j'ai gagné de l'argent en même temps!

c Il y a beaucoup de travail et ce n'est pas bien payé.

d L'après-midi, je dois préparer un repas simple pour les enfants.

e J'ai une voiture pour emmener les enfants à l'école!

f La famille a un gros chien et je déteste les animaux!

g J'ai une chambre indépendante.

h Les trois enfants n'étaient pas sages.

i Je n'ai pas vu ma famille pendant toute une année.

j J'étais libre le week-end.

Labo-langue

Negative expressions

To talk about things that do **not** happen – including **never**, **nothing**, **no more** – you must make the verb negative.

A   Learn these by heart

ne... pas	= *not*	Je **ne** mange **pas** de fruits de mer.
		= *I don't eat seafood.*
ne... rien	= *nothing*	**Je ne mange rien à midi.**
		= *I don't eat anything at midday.*
ne... jamais	= *never*	**Je ne mange jamais de viande.**
		= *I never eat meat.*
ne... plus	= *no more*	**Je ne mange plus de poisson.**
		= *I don't eat fish any more.*

B   Now use your head

Picture the two-part negative expressions above as a headset:

Je ne regarde pas le match à la télé.

Imagine the same sentence with **ne... plus** and **ne... jamais**. What do they mean?

Where a <u>noun</u> follows a negative expression, use **de** (or **d'**) instead of *un*, *une* or *des*:

Je ne mange pas **de hamburgers** et jamais **de frites**.

---

1   **Make these sentences negative. Use two different negative expressions for each.**

Example   *Je ne bois jamais de coca.*

a   Je mange.

b   Tu regardes la télé?

c   On aime la pizza.

d   Il est malade.

e   J'adore les fruits de mer.

f   Elle fait la cuisine.

2   **Now make as many different negative sentences as you can with each of these sentences.**

Example   *Il mange à la maison. →*
*Il **ne** mange **pas**.../Il **ne** mange **plus**..., etc.*

a   Je fais mes devoirs.

b   Tu regardes le film?

c   Elle prend un yaourt.

d   Je range ma chambre.

e   Il mange une banane.

f   Il fait beau en Angleterre.

3   **Complete these sentences with a negative.**

a   Tu manges souvent de la viande? Non, je ne mange...

b   On fête l'anniversaire ici? Non, on ne...

c   Il mange beaucoup au petit déjeuner? Non, il ne...

d   Tu comprends toujours quand tu es en France? Non, je...

e   Elle fait la vaisselle d'habitude? Non, elle...

f   On dîne à six heures en France? Non, on...

D **A moveable headset**

When there are two verbs together, put the negative round the first verb:

Je **ne** veux **pas** ranger ma chambre.
I don't want to tidy up my bedroom.

Tu **n'**aimes **plus** faire la cuisine?
You don't like to do the cooking any more.

It's the same in the perfect tense – put the negative round the first verb (the auxiliary):

Il **n'**a **jamais** mangé de poisson.
He has never eaten fish.

Elle **n'**a **rien** dit.
She never said anything.

 4 **Complete the sentences.**

pas	jamais	plus	rien

a Tu as toujours aimé le poisson?
  Non, je n'ai ✳ ✳ ✳ aimé le poisson.
b Tu as tout mangé?
  Non, je n'ai ✳ ✳ ✳ mangé!
c Tu as parlé à tout le monde?
  Non , je n'ai ✳ ✳ ✳ parlé à tout le monde.
d Tu as encore revu cette fille?
  Non, je n'ai ✳ ✳ ✳ revu cette fille!

 5 **Translate into English.**

a Je ne veux pas faire la vaisselle.
b Je ne vais jamais ranger ma chambre.
c Tu n'as jamais mangé de pizza?
d Il n'a rien dit.

Coping with unknown vocabulary

What happens when you don't know words, like 'coat hanger' or 'alarm clock'?

Or if you don't know the word for something you have forgotten to bring with you?

There are various strategies you can use. First, say:

- *Comment dit-on...?* (= How do you say...?)
- *Tu peux me prêter...?* (= Can you lend me...?)

Then:

a Mime: *Je mime...*

b Draw: *Je fais un dessin...*

c Define: using the word 'thingumebob / whatd'youcallit':
C'est le truc / le machin pour mettre les vêtements.

d Otherwise, use the dictionary.

Once you have found or been told the new vocabulary, repeat it two or three times to help it sink in. If necessary, ask for the spelling: *Ça s'écrit comment, "cintre"?*

---

1 Regarde les images. Écoute et relie.

Exemple **1f**

- du dentifrice • ma brosse à dents
- un cintre • un réveil
- mon inhalateur • un baladeur

SPEAKING

2 À deux: changez les parties soulignées de la conversation (gloves, towel, etc.).

A *J'ai oublié... euh, comment dit-on 'toothbrush'?*
B *Je sais pas.*
A *J'ai oublié... euh, attends, je mime...*
B *Tu as oublié ton dentrifrice?*
A *Euh... non, pas dentifrice, c'est le truc pour se laver les dents...*
B *Ah, ta brosse à dents?*
A *Oui! C'est ça. Ça s'écrit comment?*
B *B-r-o-s-s-e, brosse.*
A *Oui, j'ai oublié ma brosse à dents.*

Tu sais tout?

Écoute!

Listen and choose the correct picture.

Lis!

READING

2 **Read Alice's account of her exchange visit and find the five statements that are true.**

Alice et Shona

Je fais un échange et je passe un mois en Écosse. Je parle anglais tous les jours – c'est super! Je m'entends super bien avec Shona ma corres, et la famille est très gentille. Je l'aide un peu aussi: normalement, je fais mon lit et je débarrasse souvent la table mais je fais rarement la vaisselle et je ne fais jamais la cuisine! En général, j'aime la cuisine – la cuisine écossaise est très différente mais j'aime bien ça!

On sort souvent avec les copains de Shona. De temps en temps, on va au club des jeunes et on discute. Samedi soir, on va se retrouver au restaurant pour l'anniversaire de sa copine. Génial!

a Alice always speaks French with Shona.

b Shona is very nice.

c Alice tries to help with the housework.

d She doesn't like Scottish food.

e Alice doesn't go out with Shona's friends.

f Alice can chat with Shona and her friends at the youth club.

g It's Shona's birthday on Saturday.

h Shona and Alice are going to the restaurant with a friend on Saturday.

Parle!

SPEAKING

3 **Choose five household chores. Say something different about each of them.**

Example *Je ne range jamais ma chambre.*
Je déteste ça!

Écris!

WRITING

4 **Write five sentences about what you do to help at home.**

Example *Je range ma chambre.*

Quel dilemme!

1 Before reading the text, look at the pictures. What do you think the text is about? What could the dilemma be?

Tom est en France chez Julien Leroy, son correspondant français. Tom est assez timide.

Hier soir, ils sont allés au bowling. C'était horrible! Julien a parlé à tous ses copains et Tom n'a rien compris. Il est resté seul dans un coin. Plus tard, une super fille est arrivée.

Pendant une heure, ils ont joué et parlé.
«Audrey, je voudrais te dire que…»
À ce moment-là, Julien est arrivé. Il a embrassé Audrey.
«Ah Tom, tu connais Audrey, ma petite amie. Elle est sympa, hein?» Audrey a regardé Tom, Tom a regardé Audrey. Il était triste et déçu.

«Salut! Tu es Tom, le corrres de Julien, c'est ça? Moi, je suis Audrey!»
«Ils parlent trop vite, non?»
«Euh… oui, je ne comprends rien.»
«Ils sont nuls! Tu voudrais jouer au ping-pong avec moi?»
«Oui, je veux bien.» Tom était heureux. Audrey était si sympa, et si belle!

Ce matin, Tom a reçu un SMS d'Audrey:

«Je veux te revoir. Retrouve-moi à la sortie du collège à 17 h – mais sans Julien. Please?! Bisou*. Audrey»   *love

2 Once you have read the story, find the French for these phrases.

a Tom didn't understand a thing.
b He stayed on his own in a corner.
c For an hour…
d He kissed Audrey.
e Tom got a text message.
f Meet me…

Que faire? Tom adore Audrey et il est en France pour deux semaines… deux semaines avec Audrey!!! Mais Julien est son correspondant et il va le revoir bientôt en Angleterre.

3 Choose an ending for the story.

a Tom aime trop Audrey pour la perdre et répond: *D'accord, à 17 h! Je t'aime.*

b Tom répond: *Je t'aime mais tu dois d'abord casser avec Julien si tu veux sortir avec moi!*

c Tom répond: *Désolé, je t'aime beaucoup mais Julien est un copain. Je ne peux pas prendre sa copine.*

4 What would you do in Tom's situation?

clic-mag

Forum: nos traditions françaises

mimi6: Il y a beaucoup de fêtes et traditions françaises, mais on a oublié le vrai sens de ces traditions – c'est juste une raison pour ne pas travailler.

balou: C'est vrai. Par exemple, pour beaucoup de Français, Noël n'a plus rien à faire avec Dieu ou Jésus. C'est une occasion de manger beaucoup et d'acheter des choses inutiles*!

*useless

mwamwa: En décembre, il fait froid, il fait noir, on n'a rien à célébrer – sauf Noël! C'est génial! Ça fait du bien!

g-rezon: Je déteste Noël. On nous encourage à dépenser beaucoup d'argent.

mwamwa: Moi, j'adore Noël et j'adore recevoir et offrir des cadeaux. Je n'ai pas beaucoup d'argent, mais j'aime acheter des cadeaux.

g-rezon: Je refuse d'acheter des cadeaux à Noël. Il y a des gens qui n'ont pas d'argent et rien à manger. On doit faire plus pour eux.

 1 Read the forum. Who says the following?

a We're encouraged to spend far too much at Christmas.
b People have forgotten why we have many of our traditions.
c Christmas has nothing to do with religion any more.
d I love getting and giving presents.
e There are people who don't have money or anything to eat. We should do more for them.
f Christmas is great – it cheers you up in winter!

2 Which opinions (if any) in the forum are nearest to yours? Tell your partner what you think.

La nourriture et la boisson	**Food and drink**
du pain	bread
du fromage	cheese
du pâté	pâté
un yaourt	yoghurt
du sel	salt
du poivre	pepper
une banane	banana
une tomate	tomato
de la salade	salad, lettuce
la salade de concombre	cucumber salad
la salade de fruits	fruit salad
des chips	crisps
du steak haché	minced steak
des lasagnes	lasagne
du coca	cola
de l'eau minérale	mineral water

À table	**At the table**
Tu aimes (la salade de tomates)?	Do you like (tomato salad)?
J'aime beaucoup / J'adore ça.	I love it.
C'est délicieux / très bon.	It's delicious / very good.
Sers-toi!	Help yourself!
Tu veux (encore) de la pizza?	Do you want some (more) pizza?
Je veux bien, merci.	I'd like that, thanks.
Non merci, j'ai assez mangé.	No thanks, I'm full.
C'était délicieux.	It was delicious.
Tu peux me passer...?	Can you pass me...?
Vous pouvez me passer...?	Can you pass me...?
s'il te plaît	please
s'il vous plaît	please
poli(e)	polite
impoli(e)	impolite, rude
végétarien(ne)	vegetarian

Le négation	**The negative**
ne... pas	not
ne... rien	nothing
ne... jamais	never
ne... plus	no more

Aider à la maison	**Helping at home**
Je peux vous aider?	Can I help you?
Je peux t'aider?	Can I help you?
Je peux...	I can...
Tu peux...	You can...
faire mon lit	make my bed
faire ton lit	make your bed
ranger ma chambre	tidy my room
ranger ta chambre	tidy your room
mettre le couvert	set the table
débarrasser la table	clear the table
faire la cuisine	do the cooking
faire la vaisselle	do the washing up
passer l'aspirateur	vacuum
tous les jours	every day
d'habitude	usually
souvent	often
de temps en temps	from time to time
rarement	not often, rarely
normalement	usually, normally
en général	generally
le matin / le soir	in the mornings / evenings

La différence	**Difference**
une mobylette	moped / scooter
conduire	to drive
faire la queue	to queue

À une fête — *At a celebration*

fêter	*to celebrate*
assister à	*to go to, to be present at*
la première communion	*first communion*
faire un cadeau	*to give a present*
aider (à)	*to help (to)*
commencer (à)	*to begin (to)*
encourager (à)	*to encourage (to)*
continuer (de)	*to continue, to carry on (–ing)*
essayer (de)	*to try (to)*
finir (de)	*to finish (ing)*
oublier (de)	*to forget (to)*
refuser (de)	*to refuse (to)*

 Make up as many sentences as you can about the pictures using the words / phrases on this page.

Pourquoi apprendre le français?

Pour mieux comprendre notre monde

On peut se marier à quel âge au Maroc?

Voir page 83.

Qu'est-ce qui était différent dans les années 50?

Voir page 85.

Tu es contre la pollution? Tu es pour une vie plus écolo? Qu'est-ce qu'on peut faire?

Voir page 86.

Anthony travaille où? Qu'est-ce qu'il fait pour protéger l'environnement?

Voir page 88.

vrir le monde **5**

Comment organiser
ce que tu vas écrire?

Voir page 92.

Quel est le
problème?
Le racket: quoi
faire?

Voir page 94.

Voir page 95.

L'ozone, c'est quoi?
La réduction de la
pollution à l'ozone,
c'est possible?

À la fin de l'unité 5, reviens ici et réponds
aux questions!

J'ai le droit?

- Discussing what you are / are not allowed to do.

Je peux / Je ne peux pas:

- **a** m'habiller comme je veux.
- **b** mettre ma musique à fond.
- **c** me coucher quand je veux.
- **d** avoir un job.
- **e** sortir le soir.
- **f** avoir un ordinateur dans ma chambre.
- **g** inviter des copains chez moi.
- **h** avoir des piercings.

READING

1 Relie chaque dessin 1–4 à une des expressions a–h.

Exemple *1h Je peux avoir des piercings.*

2a Écoute Marie. Tu entends combien de fois…?

- **a** «Je peux…»
- **b** «Je ne peux pas…»

2b Réécoute. Note les lettres des expressions-clé dans l'ordre.

Exemple *c, …*

SPEAKING

3 Compare avec un(e) partenaire.

Exemple **A** *Moi, je peux m'habiller comme je veux.*
  B *Moi, aussi! Mais je ne peux pas avoir de piercings.*
  A *Moi non plus.*

WRITING

4 Résume ce que tu peux faire à la maison.

Exemple *Je peux avoir un ordinateur dans ma chambre.*
Je ne peux pas sortir le soir, sauf le samedi.

Grammaire

Use these words to emphasise the person:

je > moi	**Moi**, je peux… / **Moi** aussi!
tu > toi	**Toi**, tu peux… / **Toi** non plus!
il > lui	**Lui**, il…
elle > elle	**Elle**, elle…

À quel âge peut-on se marier?

Pays	Filles	Garçons
l'Afrique du Sud	12	14
l'Algérie	18	18
la France	18	18
la Grande-Bretagne	16	16
le Luxembourg	16	18
le Maroc	18	18
la Turquie	18	18
le Viêt Nam	18	20

READING
5a **Lis et complète.**

a En Grande-Bretagne, on peut se marier à ans.

b En France, les filles peuvent se marier à ② ans.

c Les ③ français peuvent se marier à dix-huit ans.

d En ④, les filles peuvent se marier à douze ans.

e Au Viêt Nam, les peuvent se marier à vingt ans.

5b **Écoute pour vérifier.**

WRITING
5c **Écris cinq phrases incomplètes (comme activité 5a) et échange avec un(e) partenaire.**

Exemple *En Algérie, les garçons peuvent se marier à [?] ans.*

SPEAKING
5d **Test de mémoire. A dit un pays. B ne regarde pas le livre et dit l'âge légal pour se marier. (B→A)**

Exemple **A** *À quel âge peut-on se marier au Luxembourg?*
B *Les filles peuvent se marier à 16 ans et les garçons à 18 ans.*

Grammaire

***pouvoir* + infinitive**

je peux = I can
tu peux = you can
il/elle/on peut = he/she/people can
nous pouvons = we can
vous pouvez = you can
ils/elles peuvent = they can

Grammaire

⚠️ **en** + *fem. country* (**en Algérie**, etc)
au + *masc. country* (**au Maroc**, etc)

Idées cadeaux

READING

1 Relie les photos 1–8 aux noms a–h.

READING

2 Trouve le cadeau idéal pour ces jeunes.

Exemple *a Pour Quentin, un ordinateur portable.*

a Quentin aime bien les gadgets. Il aime surfer sur Internet mais il n'a pas d'ordinateur à la maison.

b Laura adore le cinéma et elle veut regarder des films dans sa chambre.

c Maxime aime rester en contact avec ses copains mais c'est impossible en ce moment parce que son portable est cassé.

d Yasmina aime beaucoup la musique mais elle déteste chanter. Elle a déjà un baladeur MP3.

e Nicolas s'intéresse beaucoup à la photographie mais il n'a pas d'appareil.

3 Écoute (1–6) et note les deux cadeaux (a–h) que chaque jeune désire.

Exemple *1: e, h*

SPEAKING

4 En secret, A choisit ses trois gadgets préférés dans la liste. B pose des questions pour les deviner. (B→A)

Exemple **B** *Tu veux un portable?*
A *Non, j'ai déjà un portable.*
B *Tu voudrais un lecteur DVD?*
A *Oui!*

WRITING

5 Tu peux donner les cadeaux a–h à ta famille ou à tes copains. Donne les raisons pour ton choix.

Exemple *Je donne une machine à karaoké à ma grand-mère parce qu'elle adore chanter.*

Je veux / Je voudrais

a un portable
b une machine à karaoké
c un appareil photo numérique
d un lecteur DVD
e un baladeur MP3
f un clavier électronique
g une console PS3
h un ordinateur portable

je veux = *I want*
je voudrais = *I would like*
(more polite!)
To see the full pattern of the verb **vouloir**, see page 145.

Je	donne	un	portable / lecteur DVD etc.	à mon frère / père ma copine / mère
		une	console PS3 etc.	
parce qu'il/ elle	aime adore	la musique / le cinéma / la photographie regarder des films écouter de la musique surfer sur Internet		

Visit **clic!** OxBox

DANS LES ANNÉES 50...

a On écoutait des disques en vinyle sur un tourne-disque. Ma mère avait un poste de radio à transistor.

b La télévision était un luxe. Les images étaient en noir et blanc. Il y avait une seule chaîne. Je regardais Omer, le petit canard*.
*duck

c Le téléphone était grand et noir avec un cadran* rond à chiffres et à lettres. À la campagne, on devait passer par l'opératrice.
*dial

d Une nouvelle* importante ou urgente? On envoyait un télégramme: c'était le message écrit le plus rapide.
*piece of news

e Le week-end, les gens jouaient à des jeux de société, comme le Monopoly.

6a READING Lis l'article. Relie dessins 1–5 aux bulles a–e.

6b READING Lis et réponds en anglais.

a How did people listen to music in the 1950s?
b How many TV channels were there?
c How did people send messages?
d What sort of games did people play?
e What did a telephone look like?

7 READING **Grammaire: trouve dans les bulles les verbes à l'imparfait et traduis en anglais.**

Exemple *On écoutait des disques en vinyle. = People used to listen to vinyl records.*

8 READING **Relie 1–5 à une bulle.**

1 Maintenant, on a des portables pour parler, envoyer des SMS et prendre des photos et des vidéos.
2 Maintenant, il y a des consoles de jeux électroniques.

3 Maintenant, les images sont en couleur, il y a beaucoup de chaînes et il y a aussi les DVD.
4 Maintenant, on peut envoyer un email ou un SMS.
5 Maintenant, on télécharge sa musique sur un baladeur MP3.

Grammaire

The imperfect (*l'imparfait*)

The imperfect tense is used to say how things used to be:

C'était génial. = It was great.

Il y avait une seule chaîne.
= There was only one channel.

Je regardais le petit canard.
= I used to watch the little duck.

See Labo-langue, page 91.

Non à la pollution!

Talking about ways to be more environmentally friendly

a Respectez la nature.
b Recyclez les bouteilles.
c Utilisez les transports en commun.
d Économisez l'eau.

e N'utilisez pas d'aérosols au CFC.
f Ne partez pas trop souvent en avion.
g Ne laissez pas toutes les lumières allumées.
h N'utilisez pas de sacs en plastique.

Grammaire

Use the imperative to give advice, orders or instructions:

- person you say *tu* to:
  Pars! Utilise!
  Go! Use!
- person you say *vous* to:
  Recyclez! Partez!
  Recycle! Go!
- To tell someone not to do something, put *ne* (or *n'*) in front of the imperative and *pas* after it:
  Ne pars pas! Ne partez pas!
  Don't go!
  N'utilise pas! N'utilisez pas!
  Don't use!

READING

1 Trouve un conseil pour chaque dessin.

Exemple *1d, économisez l'eau*

2 Écoutez le rap et notez les conseils a–h dans l'ordre mentionné.

Visit **clic!** **OxBox**

3a **Écoute. Pierre suit les conseils a–h page 87 (✔) ou pas (✗)?**

Exemple *a* ✔

3b **Réécoute. Mets les huit questions dans l'ordre.**

Exemple *1 Tu respectes la nature?*

3c **À deux: qui est le plus écolo? A pose les questions de l'activité 3b. B donne ses réponses personnelles. Comptez vos points.**

Questions 1–4: toujours = 2, quelquefois = 1, jamais = 0
Questions 5–8: toujours = 0, quelquefois = 1, jamais = 3

4a **Lis le Forum-Internet. Résume les trois suggestions en anglais.**

1 Tu recycles les bouteilles?
2 Tu respectes la nature?
3 Tu économises l'eau?
4 Tu utilises les transports en commun?
5 Tu laisses toutes les lumières allumées?
6 Tu utilises les sacs en plastique?
7 Tu utilises des aérosols au CFC?
8 Tu pars souvent en avion?

Forum-Internet

Bastien

Bastien, Paris:
Moi, je suis pour une vie plus écolo, mais mon collège n'est pas très écolo. Qu'est-ce que vous faites dans votre collège?

Fatira, Lyon: On a planté des arbres et des fleurs dans la cour*. Je pense que c'est une bonne idée.
la cour = the playground
Manon, Céret: Au collège, on a une poubelle* spéciale dans la cour. On jette les déchets organiques (restes de fruits, sandwiches, etc) dans cette poubelle. Je suis contre le gaspillage*. *une poubelle* = a bin / *le gaspillage* = waste
Karim, Marseille: Dans mon collège, on recycle les feuilles de brouillon* et autres papiers. *les feuilles de brouillon* = rough paper

4b **Tu es pour ou contre les suggestions?**

Exemple *Je suis pour la suggestion de Karim parce que je suis contre le gaspillage. Je pense qu'il faut recycler le papier.*

Défi!

In groups of 3 or 4, think up other suggestions for a greener school (in class, at break time and in the canteen).

• Present the best suggestion to the rest of the class.

• Make a poster with your suggestion, with illustrations and a slogan.

Opinions

Je suis pour (une vie plus écolo).
= I'm for / in favour of a greener lifestyle.
Je suis contre (le gaspillage).
= I'm against (waste).
Je pense que (c'est une bonne idée). = I think (it's a good idea).
Il faut (recycler le papier).
= We should (recycle paper).

C'est la vie!

VIDEO
1a Regarde le clip <u>sans</u> le son. Décris ce qui se passe en anglais.

VIDEO
1b Regarde encore. Vrai ou faux?

Anthony travaille dans une association de protection de l'environnement.

   a Anthony works on the Naturescope website.
   b Youngsters go to the Frioul islands by train.
   c Anthony organises a cleaning operation.

READING
2 Relie les légendes aux photos.

   a Anthony travaille sur Internet.
   b On cherche les petites pièces de plastique et de verre.
   c On met les déchets dans de grands sacs.
   d Anthony donne des instructions au groupe.

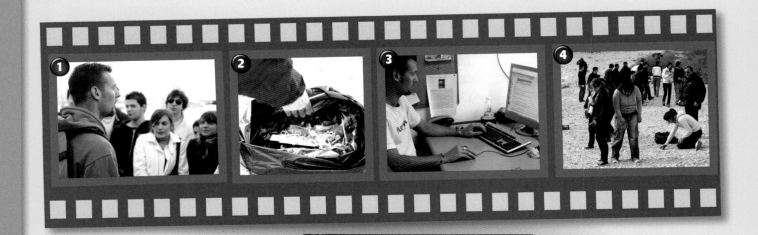

Le sais-tu?

Durée de vie des déchets

Mégot: de 1 à 5 ans

Chewing-gum: de 1 à 5 ans

Canette alu: de 10 à 100 ans

Plastique: de 100 à 1 000 ans

Visit **Clic!** **O×Box**

3a Relie l'anglais à l'équivalent en français.

a Don't waste water.
b You should put your rubbish in a bin.
c Sort your rubbish.
d You shouldn't throw papers on the ground.
e Turn off the lights.
f Recycle glass.
g Respect nature.

1 Respectez la nature.
2 Ne gaspillez pas l'eau.
3 Recyclez le verre.
4 Il ne faut pas jeter les papiers par terre.
5 Il faut mettre les déchets dans la poubelle.
6 Triez vos déchets.
7 Éteignez la lumière.

 3b Regarde. Note les conseils 1–7 dans l'ordre mentionné.

Exemple   *4, ...*

 4 Lis l'email d'Anthony. Complète les phrases a–e.

a Anthony loves...
b On the Naturscope website, there are...
c He does research and writes articles about...
d In schools, he...
e He thinks his work is important because...

La nature, c'est ma passion. Mon travail à Naturoscope, c'est d'organiser un site web avec des infos et des conseils. Je fais des recherches et j'écris des articles sur les problèmes de l'environnement et les actions écologiques possibles. Je parle aussi avec les jeunes dans les collèges. La Terre est en danger. Mon travail, c'est la protection de la planète – voilà pourquoi je trouve ça important.

 5a Réponds aux questions pour savoir si tu voudrais le travail d'Anthony. Si tu as un maximum de réponses positives, c'est possible.

a Tu aimes la nature?
b Tu as souvent fait des recherches sur Internet?
c Tu aimes écrire des articles?
d Tu veux travailler dans un bureau?
e Tu aimes parler en public?
f Tu veux travailler avec des jeunes?
g Les problèmes de l'environnement t'intéressent?

 5b On te propose de faire un stage à Naturoscope. Tu veux bien? Écris une explication. Utilise les idées a–g et tes propres idées.

Exemple   *Je voudrais bien faire un stage à Naturoscope parce que j'aime beaucoup la nature. J'ai souvent fait des recherches..., etc.*
ou
Je ne voudrais pas faire un stage à Naturoscope parce que je n'aime pas beaucoup la nature. Je déteste faire des recherches..., etc.

Labo-langue

Talking about the past

A Make sure you know useful words for talking about past events.

J'ai planté cet arbre **la semaine dernière.** *I planted this tree last week.*

Moi, j'ai planté cet arbre **il y a trente ans**. *I planted this tree thirty years ago.*

B The perfect tense (*le passé composé*)

The main tense for talking about the past is the perfect. It is used to talk about a completed action or event in the past. See Labo-langue, pages 36 and 37.

Je suis venu, j'ai vu, j'ai vaincu*!

*conquered

1 Which of these words / expressions would be used to talk about the past?

(Use the glossary on pages 146–160 to help you.)

a en 1998
b demain
c hier
d la semaine dernière
e le mois prochain
f dans trois jours
g il y a dix ans
h le week–end dernier

2a Find the right ending for each sentence. There are several possibilities.

a Je
b Tu
c Mon frère
d J'
e Max
f On

1 a parlé au prof.
2 as acheté un MP3?
3 ai regardé la télé.
4 est arrivé hier.
5 suis parti.
6 a recyclé les papiers.

2b Copy the sentences, changing the infinitive to the correct form of the perfect tense.

Example *Je [**avoir**] un piercing. > J'ai eu un piercing.*

a Max [**écouter**] la radio.
b Paul [**jouer**] au Monopoly.
c On [**envoyer**] un SMS.
d Je [**acheter**] un clavier électronique.
e Tu [**aimer**] ton cadeau?
f Je [**venir**] te voir.

Visit **Clic!** OxBox

The imperfect tense – *l'imparfait*

C *C'était* + adjective

C'était (= it was) is a useful word for describing or giving an opinion in the past. It is part of the imperfect tense (see next page).

Tu as vu le match?

Oui, c'était génial!

D The imperfect is another tense used to talk about the past:

• to give an opinion or describe what something or someone was like:

C'**était** difficile. = *It was difficult.*
Le film **était** super. = *The film was great.*
Mon frère **avait** les cheveux frisés.
= *My brother used to have curly hair.*

• to say what used to happen or what happened regularly in the past:

Je **regardais** la télé tous les soirs.
= *I used to watch TV every evening.*
Il y **avait** une seule chaîne.
= *There was only one channel.*

To form the imperfect tense:

> **j'écout**ais
> **tu écout**ais
> **il/elle/on écout**ait

3 Choose a different adjective to finish each of these sentences. Write out the sentences and then translate them into English.

Example *Je suis allé à un concert. C'était nul.*
= I went to a concert. It was rubbish.

a J'ai eu un examen. C'était...
b Ma copine a fait une tarte. C'était...
c On a visité le musée. C'était...
d J'ai pris un taxi. C'était...

e Je suis allé à Paris. C'était...

4 Pick out the imperfect tense verbs.

elle demandait   j'allais
                nous avons   tu téléphones
il s'habillait
        on est parti   elles pouvaient
vous pouvez   vous étiez
                        tu faisais   ils seront

5
Would you use the perfect or imperfect tense in these sentences?

a To tell a friend you went to the cinema yesterday.
b To say the film was interesting.
c To describe what the hero looked like.
d To say you met a friend after the film.
e To explain the sort of film you used to like when you were little.

6 Translate these sentences into English.

Example *a When I was little, I used to go to primary school.*

a Quand j'étais petit, j'allais à l'école primaire.
b Quand j'étais en France, je parlais français.
c Quand il faisait beau, on allait au parc. C'était génial.
d Quand il ne faisait pas beau, on restait à la maison.
e Nous regardions la télé ou nous écoutions la radio.
f Qu'est-ce que tu faisais quand tu étais petit?
g Quand j'avais treize ans, je ne pouvais pas sortir le soir.

Défi!

Can you give the French sentences for activity 5?

I never know where to start when we have to write in French.

What do I need to know if I want to write a letter?

Here are some tips to help you with your writing.

- Make sure you understand the task and how many words you need to write.

- Don't start writing straight away. Take a bit of time to plan.

- Start by making a list of paragraph headings. If you are writing about what you are allowed to do at home, these might be: ***vêtements / musique / sorties / copains***, etc.

- Jot down any key words or phrases you could use as a mind map. For example: ***vêtements – mes parents sont cool, je peux m'habiller comme je veux, ma mère achète mes vêtements, piercings/bijoux...***

- Make a note of how many words you plan to write for each paragraph.

- Think about the tenses you are going to use.

- Write a rough draft with the basic ideas you want to include.

- Write a second draft adding in descriptions and opinions. Link ideas together with words like ***et***, ***mais***, ***ou***, etc.

There are two different types of letter: informal (to a friend or someone your own age) and formal (if you want to make a reservation or ask an organisation for information, for example).

For both types of letter, write the name of your town and the date in the top right-hand corner:

Bradford, le 28 septembre 20XX

Informal

To start: ***Cher*** + boy's name
            Chère + girl's name
            Chers + plural noun (***amis***, etc.)

In the letter: Use ***tu*** (unless the letter is to more than one person).

To end: ***Écris-moi bientôt*** or ***Réponds-moi vite.*** ***À bientôt*** or ***Grosses bises*** or ***Bisous*** + your name

Formal

To start: ***Monsieur*** or ***Madame***
In the letter: Use ***vous***.

To end: ***Veuillez agréer, Monsieur*** (or ***Madame***), ***l'expression de mes meilleurs sentiments*** + your name

1 Write about what you do / don't do to help the environment (+/- 100 words). Look back at pages 86-87 and use the advice above. Discuss with a partner which of the tips were helpful.

2 Write a letter to a French penfriend (+/- 80 words), describing what you did last weekend.

Example   *Chère Juliette*
              J'ai passé un bon week-end. Samedi matin, j'ai fait... je suis allé(e)... etc.

Ne laissez pas toutes les lumières allumées.	*Don't leave all the lights on.*
N'utilisez pas de sacs en plastique.	*Don't use plastic bags.*
Je respecte <u>toujours</u> la nature.	*I <u>always</u> respect nature.*
Je recycle <u>quelquefois</u> les bouteilles.	*I <u>sometimes</u> recycle bottles.*
Je <u>n</u>'utilise <u>jamais</u> de sacs en plastique.	*I <u>never</u> use plastic bags.*
Moi, je suis pour (une vie plus écolo).	*I'm in favour of (a greener lifestyle).*
Je suis contre (le gaspillage).	*I'm against (waste).*
Je pense que c'est une bonne idée.	*I think it's a good idea.*
il faut recycler le papier	*We must recycle paper.*

Pour écrire une lettre (à un ami/une amie)	***To write a letter (to a friend)***
Cher + *boy's name*	*Dear...*
Chère + *girl's name*	*Dear...*
Chers + *plural noun*	*Dear...*
Écris–moi bientôt.	*Write soon.*
Réponds–moi vite.	*Write back soon.*
À bientôt	*See you soon*
Grosses bises	*Love from*
Bisous	*Love from*

(plus officiel)	***(more official)***
Monsieur	*Dear Sir*
Madame	*Dear Madam*
Veuillez agréer, Monsieur (ou Madame), l'expression de mes meilleurs sentiments	*Yours sincerely*

WRITING 1 Make up as many sentences as you can about the pictures using the words / phrases on this page.

Pourquoi apprendre le français?

Pour préparer un meilleur avenir!

Tu aimes quelles matières?

Tu as choisi tes options?

Voir page 100.

Tu voudrais être footballeur? Styliste? Pop star?

C'est quoi, le métier de rêve pour toi?

Voir page 102.

Tu fais un petit boulot?

Quel petit boulot pour Emma de Caunes et Johnny Depp?

Voir page 105.

Préparer l'avenir 6

Franck, surveillant dans un collège

Autoritaire ou tolérant?

Voir page 106.

Ton copain ne va pas en cours. Tu vas mentir pour l'aider? À toi de décider!

Voir page 112.

Comment corriger et améliorer un texte?

Voir page 110.

À la fin de l'unité 6, reviens ici et réponds aux questions!

Choisir ses études

● Choosing future studies

	lundi	mardi	mercredi	jeudi	vendredi
8 h 30	anglais	physique	EPS	permanence*	français
9 h 30	espagnol	physique	EPS	maths	français
10 h 25	Récréation				*study time
10 h 40	français	musique	maths	français	espagnol
11 h 40	permanence	anglais	histoire–géo	espagnol	biologie
12 h 35	Repas				
14 h 00	histoire–géo	français		anglais	informatique
15 h 00	EPS	technologie		arts plastiques	maths
15 h 55	Récréation				
16 h 10 / 17 h 05	biologie	maths		histoire–géo	permanence

Le sais-tu?

Le collège
la sixième (6e) = Year 7
la cinquième (5e) = Year 8
la quatrième (4e) = Year 9
la troisième (3e) = Year 10
▶ le brevet des collèges (+ / – GCSE)
Le lycée
la seconde = Year 11
la première = Year 12
la terminale = Year 13
▶ le baccalauréat (+ / – A levels)

Clément, 14 ans

A Tu es en quelle classe cette année?
Cette année, je suis en quatrième.

B Qu'est-ce que tu fais comme matières?
Je fais douze matières: français, maths, histoire–géo, anglais, espagnol, SVT (sciences et vie de la terre), sciences physiques, EPS (sport), technologie et informatique, arts plastiques et musique.

C Et l'année prochaine?
L'année prochaine, je vais être en troisième. Je vais faire les douze matières obligatoires et une option *Découverte Professionnelle*, pour découvrir le monde du travail.

 1 **Écoute et lis l'interview de Clément. Note le nom de toutes ses matières. C'est quoi en anglais?**

Exemple *anglais = English*

2 **Écoute huit élèves et regarde l'emploi du temps. Ils sont dans la classe de Clément?**

Exemple *1 Oui.*

SPEAKING **3** **À deux: choisissez un jour. Regardez l'emploi du temps.**

Exemple **B** *Le lundi à 8 h 30, il y a maths ou anglais?*
       A *Anglais.*
       B *Oui! Un point.*

WRITING **4** **Réponds aux questions de l'interview.**

A Cette année, je suis en (quatrième).
B Comme matières, je fais (maths, anglais et biologie).
C L'année prochaine, je vais être en (cinquième).
   Comme matières, je vais faire (maths,...).

Visit **Clic!** OxBox

Fleur a 14 ans. Elle est française mais elle habite en Angleterre. Elle est en Year 9.

A Qu'est-ce que tu vas faire comme matières l'année prochaine? Pourquoi?

«L'année prochaine, en Year 10, je vais faire cinq matières obligatoires: anglais, maths, sciences, éducation religieuse et informatique (en France, il y en a ①!).

Comme options, je vais faire français parce que je suis forte* en français, EPS parce que c'est ma matière préférée, biologie et chimie parce que ça m'intéresse et je suis assez bonne, physique et arts plastiques parce que j'aime bien ça. Je ne vais plus faire géographie parce que ça ne m'intéresse pas, techno parce que je déteste ça et espagnol parce que je suis trop nulle!»

*good at

B Qu'est-ce que tu voudrais faire plus tard?

«Après les GCSE (un peu3 comme le ②) je voudrais faire trois A levels: français, biologie et EPS. (Les A levels, c'est l'équivalent du ③, mais en France, il y a ④ matières obligatoires.) Plus tard, je voudrais étudier les sciences de sport.»

Le brevet des collèges est le premier examen des élèves français.

5a Lis l'interview de Fleur. Regarde page 100 et trouve les détails ①–③ sur la France. Devine ④!

5b Écoute pour vérifier.

6 Relis. C'est quelle matière?

a Fleur's good at it
b it's her favourite subject
c she's interested in it
d she likes it
e she's not interested
f she hates it
g she's no good at it

7 Écoute. Numérote les expressions dans l'ordre.

Je	vais ne vais plus	faire	(anglais) (français)	parce que	c'est ma matière préférée.
					j'aime ça. je déteste ça.
				je	suis	fort(e) bon(ne) nul(le)	en	(maths).
					ça	m'intéresse. ne m'intéresse pas.
Plus tard, je voudrais		faire	(trois) (A levels) / (GCSEs) (a BTEC in engineering)
		étudier	(la géographie) (le français)

8 Réponds aux questions (**A** et **B**). Adapte le texte de **Fleur** (garde les expressions en noir).

Métiers de rêve

● Discussing jobs you'd like to do

Il est / Elle est...

a acteur / actrice
b moniteur / monitrice d'équitation
c chanteur / chanteuse
d développeur / développeuse multimédia
e infirmier / infirmière aux urgences
f informaticien / informaticienne
g styliste
h pilote de ligne
i professeur

anglais: *I am / He is / She is a + job.*
français: Je suis / Il est / Elle est + métier.

READING
1a Relie les photos aux noms de métiers.

Exemple   *1 = c*

1b Écoute pour vérifier.

SPEAKING
2 À deux: jouez au morpion. (The first to get three in a row wins.)

Exemple   **A** *Numéro 1 = Elle est chanteuse.*
          B *Numéro 5 = Elle est styliste, etc.*

Grammaire

Job titles: masculine or feminine
Typical endings are:

♂	-eur	-t	-ier	-ien
♀	-euse	-te	-ière	-ienne

⚠ Jobs ending in -e (*dentiste*) + specific professions (*professeur*) stay the same.

Visit *Clic!* OxBox

Tu voudrais faire quel métier plus tard? Tu ne sais pas? Fais ce quiz!

Choisis ta réponse préférée.

1 Tu choisiras quelles matières au lycée?

- Je choisirai langues et histoire–géo.
- Je choisirai maths et sciences.
- Je choisirai arts ou EPS.

2 Et après le lycée?

- Je partirai un an à l'étranger.
- J'arrêterai les études.
- J'étudierai à l'université.

3 Tu continueras une langue étrangère?

- Oui, c'est important pour le travail.
- Oui, c'est essentiel pour communiquer.
- Oui, c'est utile quand on voyage.

4 Tu voudrais faire quoi plus tard?

- Je voudrais être célèbre!
- Je voudrais beaucoup voyager.
- Je voudrais aider les autres.

5 Quelles sont tes principales qualités?

- Je suis extraverti(e), dynamique et passionné(e).
- Je suis travailleur/euse, généreux/euse et organisé(e).
- Je suis aventureux/euse, actif/ive et curieux/curieuse.

Résultats:

Une majorité de
Sportif/ive ou vedette de cinéma ou de la chanson!

Une majorité de
Reporter, guide ou explorateur!

Une majorité de
Infirmier/ère ou médecin dans l'action humanitaire, comme Oxfam ou Shelter!

 3 Écoute et note les réponses de Camille au quiz.

 4 À deux: A pose les questions (1–5) à B pour vérifier. (B→A)

 5a Écoute. Qui est Camille (1 ou 2)?

 5b Recopie et complète pour Camille.

Je voudrais être **1** parce que je suis fort(e) en **2**.
Je suis **3**. J'adore **4**.
Mon rêve, c'est de **5**!

Camille, 14 ans

Grammaire

Talking about the future
How many verbs in the future tense can you spot in the quiz?
Do you know their infinitives?
See pages 144–145.

 5c Complète pour toi!

passionnée   français   sciences
les animaux   travailleuse   actrice
art dramatique
jouer Shakespeare   extravertie

● Part-time jobs and ambitions

Les petits boulots

a Je travaille dans un magasin.
b Je vends des glaces.
c Je distribue des prospectus.
d J'aide à la maison.
e Je fais des courses.
f Je fais du baby-sitting.
g Je promène des chiens.

1a Relie les photos-mystère aux petits boulots.

1b Écoute pour vérifier.

1c Réécoute. Note les opinions.

1d Écoute (1–7). Ils parlent au passé (**P**) ou au futur (**F**)?

	Passé	Présent	Futur
travailler	j'ai travaillé	je travaille	je vais travailler
faire	j'ai fait	je fais	je vais faire
vendre	j'ai vendu	je vends	je vais vendre

2 À deux: jouez avec un dé. Marquez un point par phrase correcte. Dites tous les petits boulots pour gagner!

= Parle au passé!
  J'ai promené des chiens.

= Parle au futur!
  Je vais promener des chiens.

Avant d'être une star...

Emma de Caunes

Quand elle était petite, son rêve, c'était d'être **①**. Elle détestait l'**②** mais elle a eu le bac, option cinéma. Après, elle a fait des petits boulots. Elle a travaillé dans un **③**. Elle n'aimait pas ça mais elle a gagné de l'argent pour **④**. À 16 ans, elle a fait des **⑤**. Puis, à 21 ans, elle a joué son premier grand rôle dans un **⑥** et elle est devenue une **⑦** très célèbre. Elle voudrait devenir **⑧**. Elle réussira parce qu'elle est très déterminée!

actrice ● bar ● école ● fleuriste ● film
publicités ● réalisatrice* ● voyager
*director

Emma de Caunes dans *Les Vacances de Mr Bean.*

Johnny Depp

Quand il était petit, son rêve, c'**①** d'être rockeur. À l'école, il **②** seulement la musique. Il **③** le collège à 15 ans pour jouer de la guitare dans un groupe. Il **④** des petits boulots. Il **⑤** des stylos par téléphone.

Son premier petit rôle au cinéma, c'était dans le film *Nightmare on Elm Street.* Après, il **⑥** dans une série télévisée, *21, Jump Street.* Les jeunes Américaines ont adoré!

Johnny Depp **⑦** une idole internationale. Il ne parle pas beaucoup du prochain film qu'il **⑧**.

était ● aimait ● est devenu ● a fait ● a joué
a quitté ● a vendu ● va faire

Johnny Depp et sa compagne, Vanessa Paradis, actrice et chanteuse française

READING
3 Lis les articles. Complète avec les mots dans les boîtes.

4 Écoute pour vérifier.

READING
5 Relis. C'est qui – Emma de Caunes ou Johnny Depp?

a played in a band
b passed a film studies exam
c sold pens over the phone
d worked in a bar
e wants to be a director
f he played in a TV series

SPEAKING
6 À deux: complétez l'interview d'Emma et de Johnny. (B→A)

WRITING
7 Réponds aux questions pour toi et écris une mini autobiographie.

1 **A: Quand tu étais petit(e), ton métier de rêve, c'était quoi?**
B: Quand j'étais petit(e), mon rêve, c'était d'être (acteur)...
2 **A: Tu as fait quels examens?**
B: J'ai passé...
3 **A: Tu as déjà fait des petits boulots?**
B: Oui, j'ai travaillé dans (un magasin).
4 **A: Quels sont tes projets?**
B: Je voudrais étudier / faire / être...

C'est la vie!

Voici Franck Martinez.
Il est surveillant* dans
un collège à
Marseille.

*supervisor

1 Regarde le clip. Décris ce que tu vois.

2 Lis les observations a–d et regarde le clip. Vrai ou faux?

- **a** Students wear jeans.
- **b** They don't wear trainers.
- **c** They work on computers in cover lessons.
- **d** They have a student planner.

3a Regarde. Lis ces questions posées à Franck.
Mets-les dans l'ordre du clip.

- **a** Vous êtes bien payé?
- **b** Qu'est-ce que vous voudriez faire plus tard?
- **c** En quoi consiste votre travail de surveillant?
- **d** Quelles qualités il faut avoir pour être surveillant?

devenir   cantine   autoritaire   mois   juste   éducation physique et sportive   tolérant   élèves

3b Complète les réponses de Franck avec les mots de droite.

1 Il faut être très **1** avec les enfants. Je pense qu'il faut
   être **2** avant d'être **3**.
2 Nous sommes payés 530 euros par **4**.
3 Mon travail consiste à accueillir* les **5**, à surveiller*
   les récréations et la **6**, récolter les billets d'absence* et
   faire rentrer et sortir les élèves.
4 Je voudrais **7** professeur d' **8**.

*to look after
 to supervise
 collect absence notes

3c Regarde encore pour vérifier.

Visit **clic!** OxBox

Le sais-tu?

- Supervisors (surveillants) are nicknamed 'les pions' (pawns) by French students.
- Anatole France was a famous French writer (1844–1924). A lot of French streets and schools are named after him.
- French people speak French with different accents, depending where they come from. People from Marseille, like Franck, speak French with a strong 'singing' accent. They also tend to make the 'en' sounds more like 'in' and to pronounce the final 'e' in words.

Anatole France

VIDEO

4 **Regarde la fin du clip. Complète les bulles pour Franck (photo A). Choisis ta bulle préférée.**

- **a** Mon travail, c'est très actif et très ✳✳✳!
- **b** J'aime bien mon travail, mais c'est ✳✳✳!
- **c** Le soir, je suis ✳✳✳ de rentrer!

interessant content fatigant

READING

5 **Franck explique pourquoi il est surveillant. Relie les débuts et fins de phrases.**

1 Quand j'étais petit,...

2 C'est assez bien payé et...

3 Je voudrais devenir prof alors...

a ça finance mes études.

b c'est une bonne expérience professionnelle.

c j'aimais bien l'école.

SPEAKING

6 **Tu aimerais être surveillant(e)? Pourquoi? Utilise les points 1–3 et / ou des raisons personnelles.**

Exemple *Je voudrais être surveillant(e) parce que c'est assez bien payé...*

ou

 Je ne voudrais pas être surveillant(e) parce que je ne voudrais pas travailler dans une école...

Défi!

Listen again. Explain in English:
- Franck's timetable
- what the pupils think of him

Labo-langue

Talking about the future

As in English, there is more than one way to talk about the future in French.

1   the present tense (*le présent*)

for something that is certain to happen very soon:
Demain, je commence mon petit boulot.
= *I'm starting my job tomorrow.*

2   *aller* + infintive
to talk about something that is <u>going to happen</u> in the near future:
L'année prochaine, je vais apprendre le chinois.
= *I'm going to learn Chinese next year.*

3   *Je voudrais* + infinitive
to express a wish, something you would like to happen in the future, but which is not certain:
Je voudrais être actrice.
= *I would like to be an actress.*

4   the future tense (*le futur*)
to talk about what <u>will happen</u>, particularly in the distant future
Tu partiras à l'étranger après ton bac?
= *Will you go abroad after your A levels?*

You can easily recognise the future tense of regular verbs by the endings: they are almost the same as the present tense of *avoir*:

**je travaillerai
tu travailleras
il/elle/on travaillera**

Some verbs are irregular:
Je serai = *I will be*   **J'aurai** = *I will have*
Je ferai = *I will do*

See Grammar pages 139–140 for more about the future tense.

1   Which group (1-4) do these sentences belong to?

a Je voudrais aller en France.
b Plus tard, je ne travaillerai pas dans un magasin.
c Je vais aller à l'université.
d Ce soir, je fais mes devoirs après le dîner.

2a   Copy the sentences with the correct form of *aller*.

a Je ✳✳✳ téléphoner à ma copine en France.
b Tu ✳✳✳ continuer la géo?
c Mon frère ✳✳✳ faire du baby-sitting demain soir.
d On ✳✳✳ réviser de la grammaire.
e Tu ✳✳✳ faire un petit boulot pendant les vacances?
f Qu'est-ce qu'il ✳✳✳ faire demain?

2b   Translate the sentences in activity 2a into English.

3   Pick out the future tense verbs.

elle regardera	je choisis
elle choisira	tu téléphones
tu as continué	il regarde
on est partis	je continuerai
tu téléphoneras	on partira

4   Translate into English these predictions which contain future tense verbs.

Exemple   **a** *I will speak 3 languages.*

a Je parlerai trois langues.
b Tu partiras à l'étranger.
c Elle voyagera dans le monde entier.
d Nous gagnerons beaucoup d'argent.
e Vous finirez vos études à New York.
f Ils habiteront à Paris.

Visit *Clic!*

Using different tenses

a imperfect

*À l'école primaire
je travaillais bien!*
je travaill**ais**
tu travaill**ais**
il / ell / on travaill**ait**

b perfect

*L'année dernière,
j'ai bien travaillé!*
j'**ai** travaill**é**
tu **as** travaill**é**
il / ell / **a** travaill**é**

c present

*Cette année, je travaille
bien!*
je travaill**e**
tu travaill**e**
il / elle / on travaill**e**

d future with *aller* + infinitive

*L'année prochaine,
je vais bien travailler.*
je **vais** travailler
tu **vas** travailler
il / elle / on **va** travailler

e real future

*Plus tard, je ne
travaillerai pas... les
élèves travailleront!*
je travaill**erai**
tu travaill**eras**
il / elle / on travaill**era**

5 Match each tense on the left with its definition below.

Example *1 = c*

1 describes what is happening now or happens regularly
2 describes what used to happen or was happening
3 describes what has happened
4 describes what will happen soon
5 describes what will happen at some point in the future

6a Decide which tense is used in these sentences.

> Look out for time phrases. They can help!

1 Il <u>est allé</u> au bord de la mer pendant les vacances.
2 Je <u>mange</u> une glace.
3 Quand j'<u>étais</u> petit, je <u>jouais</u> du piano tous les jours.
4 Ma grand-mère <u>était</u> professeur de maths.
5 J'<u>ai visité</u> Paris l'année dernière.
6 Tu <u>vas faire</u> quelles matières en option l'année prochaine?
7 Le prof me <u>donne</u> des devoirs tous les jours.
8 Un jour, j'<u>habiterai</u> dans une grande maison au bord de la mer!

6b Translate the sentences (1–8) into English.

Example *He went to the seaside during the holidays.*

clic-forum Writing (2)

> The teacher told me to check my written work. But how do I do that?

> I'm supposed to improve my written work but I don't know how. It looks good as it is!

Once you've checked that there are no mistakes, read through again and think of what you can add. For instance:

J'ai un chat.

add one or two adjectives:
J'ai un petit chat roux.

add connectives:
J'ai un petit chat roux et il s'appelle Sylvestre.

et mais
parce que
ou

In Clic! 1, you learnt the SAGA strategy:

S (spelling) **A** (accents) **G** (gender) **A** (agreement)
When re-reading your French work, also remember:

Capitals: none for days, months, languages, nationality adjectives
lundi, février, français, allemand

Little words: agree with nouns:
du / de la / des; mon / ma / mes

Word order: French adjectives come after the nouns, except a few:
*un **petit** chien **noir***

Making things negative:
two parts on either side of the verb:
*je **ne** parle **pas**; elle **n'**écoute **plus***

Verbs: is it the right tense? the correct ending?

if there are two verbs **together** in the sentence, is the second one an infinitive?
*j'aime **chanter**; tu vas **partir***

Écoute!

1a Listen and select a symbol for each speaker.

Example *1 = a*

 1 a 3ème **b** 4ème

 2 a  **b**

3 a   **4 a** ✓ **5 a**   **6 a**

b   **b**   **b** ✗ **b**   **b**

Lis!

READING 2 Read the article. Select the correct option to make the sentences true.

Example *1 = 15*

1 Lucie's first dream was to be <u>a boxer / a stewardess</u>.

2 Lucie started boxing at <u>12 / 15</u>.

3 She went to a sports academy <u>instead of / after she finished</u> school.

4 She's very sporty <u>and / but not</u> very hard-working.

5 Lucie <u>is / isn't</u> aware that her boxing career will be short.

6 She's planning a career in <u>sports management / childcare</u>.

Lucie Bertaud, championne de France de boxe anglaise

À 12 ans, son rêve, c'était d'être hôtesse de l'air parce qu'elle aimait voyager mais à 15 ans, elle a découvert la boxe. Après ça, son rêve, c'était d'être championne de boxe!

Après l'école, elle est allée dans une grande école de sport.

Lucie est sportive et passionnée de boxe mais elle est aussi très sérieuse et très travailleuse. Elle sait qu'elle ne peut pas boxer très longtemps. Elle fait des études de management du sport.

Plus tard, elle voudrait être manager d'un centre sportif et avoir des enfants.

Écris!

WRITING 3 Write a paragraph about yourself giving the following information.

Example *1 Je suis en quatrième, au collège d'Ashton-on-Sea.*

1 name of school and the year you're in *Je suis en... à / au...*

2 the subjects you're best at *Je suis fort(e) en...*

3 the options you've chosen for next year *Je vais faire...*

4 the job you've always dreamt of doing *Je voudrais être...*

5 a part-time job you have done or would like to do *J'ai travaillé dans... Je voudrais...*

Parle!

SPEAKING 4 You are being interviewed by the careers officer. Read the questions and give your answers.

Example *Je suis travailleur et organisé.*

– Quelles sont tes qualités? *Je suis...*

– Qu'est-ce que tu aimes comme matières? *J'aime...*

– Tu as déjà fait un petit boulot? *Oui, j'ai travaillé...*

– Pour toi, le métier de rêve, c'est quoi? *Mon métier de rêve, c'est...*

– Qu'est-ce que tu voudrais faire plus tard? *Je voudrais...*

– Quels sont tes projets pour après le lycée? *Je vais...*

Quel dilemme!

Théo, le copain de Louis, est absent. Hier soir, Louis a téléphoné: sa mère a dit qu'il était malade.

Cet après-midi, Louis doit aller chez le dentiste. Il y va en voiture avec sa mère. Et là, devant le centre commercial, il voit... Théo. Il distribue des prospectus! Louis ne dit rien à sa mère. Il va parler à Théo ce soir.

Le soir, Louis téléphone à Théo.

«Tu étais en ville cet après-midi? Tu n'es pas malade?»

«Euh... non, mais tu ne dis rien, d'accord? Tu es mon copain, tu peux garder un secret?»

«Oui, bien sûr!»

«Je ne vais pas en cours demain. Je fais un petit boulot en ville pour gagner de l'argent. Quand les profs font l'appel*, dis 'présent' pour moi.»   *call the register

«Non, Théo! Tu ne peux pas faire ça! On a un test de maths!»

«Bof... Je suis nul en maths! Et j'ai besoin d'argent.

Louis continue:
«Mais ne veux pas mentir* pour toi!»   *to lie

«Tu ne veux pas m'aider? Tu n'es pas un vrai ami.»

Le lendemain matin, Théo n'est pas à l'école. Le prof de maths fait l'appel.

«Étienne?» «Présent.» «Amina?» «Présente.» «Louis?» «Présent.» «Théo? Théo...?»

1 Read and find the French for:

a ill
b he says nothing
c to earn money
d to call the register
e to bunk off lessons
f I need money
g to make fun of
h if I lie

2 Answer the questions.

a Why is Louis surprised to see Théo in town?
b What are Théo's reasons for bunking off?
c What is Théo asking Louis to do?

3 What advice would you give Louis?

a Écoute Théo. Un copain, c'est plus important que l'école!
b N'écoute pas Théo. Il doit aller à l'école.
c Parle discrètement au prof et explique la situation.

clic-mag

Ici, on parle français!

Cinq *mauvaises* raisons pour ne pas apprendre le français!

1 C'est trop dur et ça prend trop de temps.

2 Tout le monde parle anglais.

3 Ce n'est pas intéressant.

4 Je n'habiterai jamais en France.

*I won't need

a Regarder des films, écouter des chansons, jouer à des jeux, surfer sur Internet, voyager, se faire des amis, c'est intéressant, non? En français, c'est super parce que c'est une culture nouvelle.

b Les top footballeurs ont travaillé longtemps sur un terrain de foot pour être champions! Les langues, c'est comme le foot, il faut du temps!

c Il y a besoin de linguistes dans le tourisme, les loisirs, les affaires*, le marketing, les médias, le commerce, etc. On gagne plus d'argent (de 8 à 20%) quand on parle une langue étrangère.

*business

d Plus de 128 millions de personnes parlent français dans 40 pays sur les cinq continents! Tu rêves d'habiter sur une île des Caraïbes? Apprends le français!

e L'anglais, c'est la langue maternelle de seulement 6,5% de la population mondiale. 75% des gens dans le monde ne parle pas un mot d'anglais!

READING
1a Read and match the (bad) reasons not to learn French (1-5) to the reasons why it is important (a-e).

SPEAKING
1b Explain each one in English.

SPEAKING
2 In pairs, find arguments to convince someone (in English) who wants to drop French not to.

6.8 Vocabulaire

Le collège et le lycée	**Secondary school**
Je suis en...	I'm in...
sixième	Year 7
cinquième	Year 8
quatrième	Year 9
troisième	Year 10
seconde	Year 11
première	Year 12
terminale	Year 13
le brevet des collèges	exam similar to GCSEs
le baccalauréat	exam similar to A levels

Les matières	**School subjects**
Qu'est-ce que tu fais / as comme matières?	What subjects do you do?
Je fais... / J'ai...	I do... / I have...
français	French
maths	maths
histoire	history
géographie	geograhy
anglais	English
espagnol	Spanish
allemand	German
SVT (sciences et vie de la terre)	biology
sciences physiques	physics
EPS (sport)	PE
technologie	design and technology
arts plastiques	art
musique	music
éducation religieuse	RE
informatique	ICT
Je vais faire + matière parce que...	I'll take + subject because...
Je ne vais plus faire + matière parce que...	I won't take + subject because
...c'est ma matière préférée	it's my favourite subject
...j'aime ça	I love it
...je déteste ça	I hate it
...je suis fort(e)	I'm good at it
...je suis nul(le)	I'm useless at it

...ça m'intéresse	I'm interested
...ça ne m'intéresse pas	I'm not interested

Mes projets	**My plans**
Qu'est-ce que tu voudrais faire plus tard?	What would you like to do later?
Quels sont tes projets?	What are your plans?
Plus tard, je voudrais...	Later, I'd like...
partir à l'étranger	to go abroad
arrêter les études	to leave school
étudier à l'université	to go to university

Un métier de rêve	**A dream job**
Tu voudrais faire quel métier plus tard?	What job would you like to do later?
Quand tu étais petit(e), ton métier de rêve, c'était quoi?	What was your dream job when you were little?
Quand j'étais petit(e), mon rêve, c'était d'être...	When I was little, I dreamed of becoming a...
Je suis / Il / Elle est + métier	I am / He / She is a / an + job
acteur / actrice	actor / actress
moniteur / monitrice d'équitation	horse-riding instructor
chanteur / chanteuse	singer
développeur / développeuse multimédia	video game designer
infirmier / infirmière aux urgences	A & E nurse
informaticien / informaticienne	computer programmer
styliste	fashion designer
pilote de ligne	airline pilot
professeur	teacher
médecin	doctor
sportif / sportive	sportsman / woman
vedette de cinéma	movie star
reporter	reporter
guide	guide
explorateur	explorer

Les qualités	**Qualities**
dynamique	energetic
passionné(e)	passionate
extraverti(e)	extrovert
organisé(e)	organised

travailleur / euse	*hard-working*
généreux / euse	*generous*
aventureux / euse	*adventurous*
curieux / curieuse	*inquisitive*
actif / ive	*active*

Les petits boulots / *Part-time jobs*

Je travaille dans un magasin.	*I work in a shop.*
Je vends des glaces.	*I sell ice cream.*
Je distribue des prospectus.	*I hand out leaflets.*
J'aide à la maison.	*I help with housework.*
Je fais des courses.	*I go shopping.*
Je fais du baby-sitting.	*I babysit.*
Je promène des chiens.	*I walk dogs.*
Tu as déjà fait des petits boulots?	*Have you already had a part-time job?*
Oui, j'ai travaillé / fait...	*Yes, I have worked / done...*

 WRITING 1 Make up as many sentences as you can about the pictures using the words / phrases on this page.

Luc sort avec Pénélope, Léo avec Claire et Kévin avec Marina.

Il/Elle est...
assez / très
grand(e), petit(e), gros(se), mince

Il/Elle a...
les cheveux blonds/bruns/roux
les cheveux longs/courts/raides/frisés
les yeux marron/bleus/verts/gris

Il/Elle porte...
un T-shirt, une chemise, un sweat, un pull
un pantalon, un jean, une jupe, une robe

rouge jaune vert(e) marron
bleu(e) noir(e) blanc(he) gris(e)

SPEAKING

1a **Can you guess who is who? Work out which boy (1-3) goes out with which girl (A-C).**

1b **Listen and match each person to his/her name. Read the caption. Did you guess the couples correctly?**

WRITING

2 **Pretend you'd like to go out with one of the people in the picture. Write a description of him/her. Read it to your partner: can he/she work out who it is?**

Example **A** _Je voudrais sortir avec un garçon grand et mince. Il a les cheveux bruns, longs et frisés. Il porte..._

En plus

1 **À une fête, tu vois un garçon/une fille sympa.**

  a Tu lui parles immédiatement.
  b Tu le/la regardes toute la soirée.
  c Tu ne lui parles pas.

2 **Pendant la fête,**

  a tu lui demandes son numéro de portable.
  b tu lui donnes ton adresse email.
  c tu le/la filmes discrètement avec ton portable.

3 **À la fin de la fête,**

  a tu l'invites à aller au cinéma.
  b tu lui dis: «À bientôt, j'espère!»
  c tu ne lui dis rien*.   *nothing

4 **Tu voudrais inviter ton nouvel ami/ta nouvelle amie chez toi.**

  a Tu lui téléphones de ton portable.
  b Tu le/la contactes sur MSN.
  c Tu lui envoies un SMS.

5 **Quand il/elle est chez toi, tes copains arrivent.**

  a Tu leur présentes ton nouvel ami/ta nouvelle amie.
  b Tu leur dis de revenir plus tard*.   *to come back later
  c Tu ne veux pas les voir!

Results

You have mostly 'a's:
It is speed-flirt for you! Be careful. you don't go too fast!

You have mostly 'b's:
Great, you take your time, slowly but surely.

You have mostly 'c's:
You are a shy romantic. Be a bit more daring!

 1a **Read the five quiz questions. Look up a maximum of four words you don't understand.**

 1b **Do the quiz. Do you agree with the result it gives you?**

Grammaire

Object pronouns

These replace nouns you don't want to repeat.
There are two types: direct and indirect.
Direct: verb + direct object
Je vois **le garçon**. = Je **le** vois.
Je vois **la fille**. = Je **la** vois.
Je vois **les copains**. = Je **les** vois.

Indirect: verb + **à** + indirect object.
Je parle **au garçon**. = Je **lui** parle.
Je parle à **la fille**. = Je **lui** parle.
Je parle **aux copains**. = Je **leur** parle.

Encore

Jeu-test!
Quel genre de sportif / sportive es-tu?

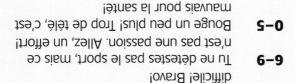

On va voir le match samedi après-midi?

a Bof, non!

b Je préfère le voir en direct à la télé.

c Samedi? Impossible. J'ai un cours de tennis.

Qu'est-ce que tu fais ce soir?

a Je regarde la télé, comme d'habitude.

b Il y a une bonne émission de sport à la télé.

c Je joue au basket au centre sportif.

Tu veux venir faire un footing avec moi?

a Ah oui, je veux bien. Bonne idée!

b Un footing? Mais pourquoi?

c Ah non, je vais rater* mon feuilleton préféré!

*to miss

Les sports d'hiver, ça te dit?

a L'hiver, la neige, le froid, beurk!

b J'aime bien regarder le ski à la télé.

c Mon rêve, c'est d'aller sur les pistes*!

*slopes

Tu fais quoi pour être en forme?

a Je fais du sport trois fois par semaine et des compétitions le week-end.

b Je vais partout à pied ou à vélo.

c Je fais EPS au collège. C'est obligatoire.

Compte tes points

1	a 0	b 1	c 3
2	a 0	b 1	c 3
3	a 3	b 0	c 0
4	a 0	b 1	c 3
5	a 3	b 1	c 0

10–15 Plus sportif/sportive que toi, c'est difficile! Bravo!

6–9 Tu ne détestes pas le sport, mais ce n'est pas une passion. Allez, un effort!

0–5 Bouge un peu plus! Trop de télé, c'est mauvais pour la santé!

---

1 Do the quiz in pairs. **A:** ask the question. **B:** choose the answers that apply to you. Count the points. (B→A)

2 Write three answers for each of the following questions. Then in pairs, take it in turns to ask and answer the questions.

Tu veux jouer au rugby avec moi?

On va voir le match de tennis?

Qu'est-ce que tu fais le samedi?

Visit Clic!

En plus

1a Match the beginnings and endings of the sentences.

Example *1C*

1 Les séries et les émissions musicales sont		**A** télé-réalité sont nulles.
2 Les émissions de		**B** sont idiots.
3 À mon avis, les feuilletons		**C** ennuyeuses.
4 J'ai horreur des		**D** jeux télévisés.
5 Les dessins		**E** animés sont très marrants.
6 Il y a trop		**F** de publicités.

1b **Rewrite the six sentences and change the adjectives to show what you think.**

Example   *1 Les séries et les émissions musicales sont intéressantes.*

> intéressant(e)
> nul(le)
> idiot(e)
> ennuyeux
> marrant(le)

1c **In pairs, swap opinions on TV programmes.**

Example **A** *Je trouve les documentaires intéressants. Et toi?*
         B *Moi, non. Je trouve, les documentaires ennuyeux.*

2a **Read Léo's account of his match last Saturday. Answer the questions in English.**

1 What did Léo do last Saturday?
2 When did he get up?
3 What did he do at 8.30?
4 How long did he warm up for?
5 How was the match?
6 Did he win or lose?
7 What did he do afterwards?

2b **Read Léo's account of his match last Saturday, then listen to Alisonne talking about her match day. Spot the seven differences between the two texts.**

Example   *1 womens championship.*

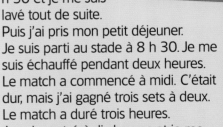
Léo

Samedi dernier, j'ai joué en finale du championnat de tennis hommes. Je me suis levé à 7 h 30 et je me suis lavé tout de suite. Puis j'ai pris mon petit déjeuner. Je suis parti au stade à 8 h 30. Je me suis échauffé pendant deux heures. Le match a commencé à midi. C'était dur, mais j'ai gagné trois sets à deux. Le match a duré trois heures. Je suis rentré à dix heures et je me suis couché tout de suite.

Planète Sauvage, le safari parc, entre Nantes et Noirmoutier

http://www.planetesauvage.com/vf/accueil.htm

Planète Sauvage

Planète Sauvage, le safari parc,
entre Nantes et Noirmoutier

English version

Vente en ligne, cliquez ici
ACHETEZ VOS BILLETS !

ACTU

L'éléphant, l'animal du mois
en savoir +

Ouverture le 1er mars 2008
Consulter notre calendrier
jour par jour...
**Nous sommes ouverts
le 24 mars**
en savoir +

fermer

venez jouer !

Piste Safari
10 km de rencontres insolites

Raid 4x4 et Km 5
En plein cœur de la savane !

Village de Brousse
L'aventure continue

Bivouac au Safari
Une nuit complète au cœur du parc !

Accueil   Actualités   Plan du Parc   Groupes & Scolaires   Infos Pratiques   Presse & Partenaires   Jeux   Contact

Si le site ne s'affiche pas veuillez télécharger le plug-in flash en cliquant ici

Les horaires d'ouverture:
(du 9 juillet au 19 août) 9 h 30 – 17 h 30
Prix:
17 euros/adulte
11 euros/enfants 4–14 ans inclus

READING
1 Read the website page. What is *Planète Sauvage*?

READING
2a Read all the information and find the missing words in the conversation.

Example *1 la Planète Sauvage*

> Vous pouvez me recommander une visite?
> Vous pouvez visiter [1].
> C'est où?
> C'est entre [2] et [3].
> Ça ouvre à quelle heure?
> Ça ouvre à [4].
> Ça ferme à quelle heure?
> Ça ferme à [5].
> Ça coûte combien?
> C'est 6 euros pour un adulte et 11 euros pour [7].
> Qu'est-ce qu'on y fait?
> Il y a une piste safari, un raid 4 x 4 et [8].

2b Listen to check your answers.

SPEAKING
3 Act out the conversation with a partner.

WRITING
4 Adapt the conversation to write about a place of interest in your area.

Visit **Clic!** OxBox

En plus

Une visite, ça s'organise

A group of French teenagers is coming to spend a week in your area. Your task is to prepare a programme of visits for them. Work in pairs or small groups.

Suggest places to go and things to do.

Example **A** *Je propose une visite au musée des transports.*
            B *Oui, bonne idée.*

Make a list of the most interesting suggestions.

Each person writes a detailed programme for Saturday and Sunday, including times and means of transport.

> SAMEDI
> De 8 h à 9 h: petit déjeuner
>
> De 9 h à 11 h 30: voyage à Édimburg (en car) et visite du château
>
> De 11 h 30 à 12 h 30: promenade dans le Royal Mile (à pied)
>
> De 12 h 30 à 13 h: déjeuner
>
> De 13 h à 15 h: visite du parlement écossais, etc.

Je propose une visite à...	I suggest visiting...
On pourrait (aller au bowling).	We could (go bowling).
On va (au château)?	Shall we go (to the castle)?
Oui, bonne idée.	Yes, good idea.
Non, ce n'est pas très intéressant.	No, that's not very interesting.
Je préfère...	I prefer...
Le centre commercial est plus intéressant que le musée.	The shopping centre is more interesting than the museum.

Take turns to read out your programme. The others make comments / criticisms.

Example *Le déjeuner n'est pas assez long.*
              La visite du parlement est trop longue.
              Ils n'ont pas assez de temps pour voir les magasins, etc.

Compare programmes. Agree the best final programme (combining bits from different programmes) and write it out.

> **Assez** and **trop**
> with adjectives
> **assez long** = long enough
> **trop long** = too long
> with nouns
> **assez de temps** = enough time
> **trop de temps** = too much time

Défi!

Write an email to explain the programme to the French teenagers. Include as much detail as possible.

Example *Après le déjeuner, vers 13 heures, on va visiter le parlement écossais. C'est un bâtiment moderne...*

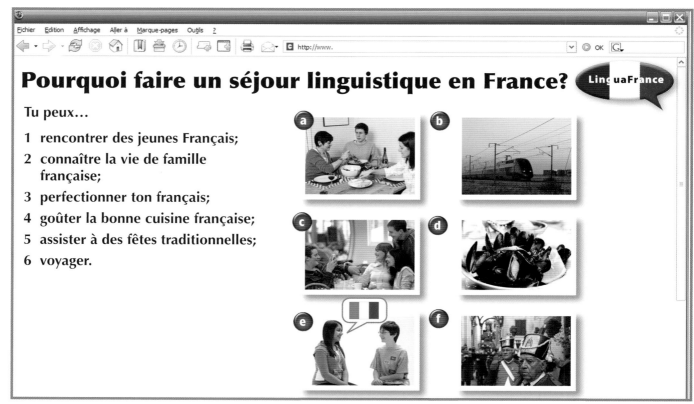

Pourquoi faire un séjour linguistique en France? LinguaFrance

Tu peux…

1 rencontrer des jeunes Français;
2 connaître la vie de famille française;
3 perfectionner ton français;
4 goûter la bonne cuisine française;
5 assister à des fêtes traditionnelles;
6 voyager.

READING

1a **Look at the web page. What is it advertising?**

READING

1b **Match the reasons (1–6) to the pictures (a–f).**

Exemple   *1 c*

READING

2a **Put the answers in the correct order to complete the interview.**

Questions	Réponses
1 Tu as passé combien de temps en France?	a On m'a invité a des fêtes traditionnelles. Je n'avais jamais fait ça avant.
2 La famille était gentille?	b Oui, elle est très bonne. Mon plat préféré, c'est les moules marinière.
3 Tu aimes la cuisine française?	
4 Qu'est-ce que tu as fait, par exemple?	c On peut voyager un peu plus et, bien sûr, on peut perfectionner son français!
5 Quels sont les avantages d'un séjour linguistique?	d J'ai passé un mois dans une famille française.
	e Oh, oui, elle était super!

2b **Listen to check your answers.**

SPEAKING

2c **In pairs: act out the conversation.**

WRITING

3 **Look at the web page again, putting in order of importance (in your opinion) reasons 1–6. Using your list, write down why you want to spend time in France.**

Example   *Je veux passer un mois en France. Je veux goûter à la bonne cuisine française. Je veux aussi…*

Visit Clic! OxBox

Le ménage? Une bonne affaire!

«Mes amis et moi, on contacte les parents de copains et on propose notre aide pour le ménage. On offre de faire un peu de ménage et la cuisine.

Ils nous donnent 8 euros par personne par heure. Ça, c'est bien!

Max fait le ménage et range la maison, Seydi passe l'aspirateur et il fait les lits. Moi, je fais la cuisine et je mets le couvert.

Par contre, on ne débarrasse pas la table et on ne fait pas la vaisselle.

On doit rentrer faire nos devoirs!»

Léa, 15 ans.

 READING

1 **Read the text. Are the following sentences true (T), false (F) or not mentioned (N)?**

a   Léa, Max and Seydi are friends.
b   They do housework to earn money.
c   Housework at their friends' houses is not well paid.
d   Max doesn't do the housework in his home.
e   Seydi never uses the vacuum cleaner.
f   He doesn't like doing the housework.
g   Léa does the cooking at her friends'.
h   Seydi often clears the table and sometimes makes the beds.
i   No one does the washing up.
j   After the housework, Léa, Max and Seydi don't have any homework to do.

SPEAKING

2a **In groups of three, organise a 'housework team'. Who does what?**

Example   **A**   *Tu passes l'aspirateur?*
          B   *Ah non, je déteste ça.*
          C   *Moi, j'aime bien. Alors je passe l'aspirateur.*

Le jeu des questions

Départ

1 Tu recycles toujours les bouteilles?

2 Tu recycles le papier?

3 Tu recycles les canettes*?

*drink cans

4 Tu respectes toujours la nature?

5 Tu utilises les transports en commun?

10 Tu es membre d'une organisation écolo?

9 Tu refuses les sacs en plastique?

8 Tu as un vélo?

7 Tu prends souvent l'avion?

6 Tu utilises les aérosols au CFC?

11 Tu vas à l'école à pied de temps en temps?

12 Tu laisses les lumières allumées?

13 Tu économises l'eau?

14 Tu es contre le gaspillage*?

*waste

15 Tu es pour une vie plus écolo?

1 Read the questions. Which are about travel and transport?

2 Listen. Who gives the more environmentally friendly answer to the question: Amélie (**A**) or Bruno (**B**)?

Example *1A*

3 Play with a partner. You need a die and a small counter each.

A throws the die and moves his / her counter round the board.
B reads out the question and A must answer. Score points for each answer:

toujours = 3 points;   souvent = 2 points;
de temps en temps = 1 point;   jamais = 0 point

Then B throws the die and moves his / her counter, etc.

Example   **A** *(throws the die) Trois!*
          B *Trois... Tu recycles les canettes?*
          A *Oui, je recycle toujours les canettes.*
          B *OK, trois points!*

4 Write your answers to the 15 questions.

souvent = *often*
Je recycle souvent les canettes.
toujours = *always*
Je recycle toujours les canettes.
de temps en temps = *sometimes*
Je recycle les canettes de temps en temps.
jamais = *never*
Je ne recycle jamais les canettes.

Visit *Clic!* OxBox

En plus
C'était vraiment comme ça?

Regarde la page 116 pour t'aider.

READING

1 Which of the expressions in the list on the right would be useful for describing the picture above?

SPEAKING

2 **A** describes the appearance of one of the people in the picture and **B** points to the right person. Regarde la page 116 pour t'aider. (**B→A**)

Example *Il est petit. Il est assez gros. Il est blond. Il a les cheveux longs et frisés.*

SPEAKING

3 **A** describes what one of the people is doing and **B** points to the right person. (**B→A**)

Example *Elle fait du vélo.*

Il / Elle...

porte des lunettes
joue du piano
écoute de la musique
surfe sur Internet
téléphone avec un portable
regarde la télévision
part en avion
utilise un aérosol
écrit une lettre
joue à des jeux de société
joue avec un chien
fait du vélo
lit le journal

Encore

Le curriculum vitae (CV)

A CV is an important document as it introduces who you are to a potential employer. Clément is working on his CV.

READING 1 Read Clément's CV and match each heading (a–h) to the information.

Exemple *a 2*

a adresse, téléphone, email
b nationalité
c langues étrangères
d expérience professionnelle
e âge
f nom et prénom
g éducation
h qualités personnelles

WRITING 2 Look at Fleur's details and fill in her CV.

Curriculum Vitae

1 _____
   FOURNIER   Clément

2 _____
   33, rue de Malte, 75011 Paris
   01 45 33 24 87
   clementfournier@hotmail.com

3 _____
   14 ans, né le 28 mai 199X

4 _____
   Français

5 _____
   élève de quatrième; prépare le brevet des collèges pour l'année prochaine

6 _____
   anglais, espagnol

7 _____
   a distribué des prospectus et des journaux

8 _____
   dynamique, travailleur, organisé

Fleur Destienne

*14 ans

*Française

*27 Gray's Inn Road, Londres
  0207 444 35 67
  fleurdestienne@hotmail.com

*sociable, travailleuse, dynamique

*anglais, français, espagnol

*en Year 9 (quatrième); prépare les GCSE (brevet des collèges) pour l'année prochaine

*baby-sitting, aide à la maison

Remember!
In French official documents, the surname usually comes first.

WRITING 3 Write your own CV using Clément's as a model.

Visit Clic! OxBox

La lettre de motivation

Magasin de jouets recherche vendeur/vendeuse

avec ou sans expérience
(samedi uniquement)

Envoyer CV et lettre de motivation à
Jeu d'Enfant
14, rue St Ernestin
75 017 Paris

Bar à jus de fruits recherche serveur ou serveuse

avec ou sans expérience
(week-ends uniquement)
Envoyer CV et lettre de
motivation à
**Fruibar
76, avenue Jean-Jaurès
75019 Paris**

Clément FOURNIER
33, rue de Malte
750 11 Paris
tél: 01 45 33 24 87
clementfournier@hotmail.com

Fruibar
76 avenue Jean-Jaurès
75019 Paris

Paris, le 17 juin

READING
1 Read the ads and find:

- **a** waiter / waitress; salesman / saleswoman
- **b** to look for
- **c** to send
- **d** letter of application
- **e** with or without experience

READING
2 Read Clément's letter. Fill in [1]–[7] with the details on his CV (Encore, page 126).

WRITING
3 Write Fleur's letter of application to *Jeu D'Enfant*. Use Clément's letter as a model.

WRITING
4 Choose an ad and write your letter of application.

Monsieur, Madame,

Je suis intéressé par la position de [1].
Je joins mon CV. Je pense avoir les qualités nécessaires pour le poste.
Je suis [2], [3] et [4]. Je parle [5] et [6].
J'ai une expérience professionnelle: j'ai [7].
Je suis libre le week-end.

Veuillez agréer, Madame, Monsieur, l'expression de mes meilleurs sentiments.

C. Fournier

Grammaire

Introduction

Here is a summary of the main points of grammar covered in *Clic! 1, 2* and *3* with some activities to check that you have understood and can use the language accurately.

Where to find information on the rules of grammar:

1	Nouns and determiners	129
2	Adjectives	130
3	The possessive	131
4	Prepositions	132
5	Pronouns	133
6	Verbs	133
7	Negatives	139
	Answers to grammar activities	140
	Verb tables	141

Glossary of terms

noun   *un nom* = a person, animal, place or thing
Mon **copain** prend le train à la **gare.**

determiner   *un déterminant* = a little word before a noun to introduce it
le chien, **un** chat, **du** jambon, **mon** frère

singular   *le singulier* = one of something
Le chien mange **un biscuit**.

plural   *le pluriel* = more than one of something
Je recycle **les papiers.**

pronoun   *un pronom* = a little word used instead of a noun or name
Il mange un biscuit. **Elles** jouent au football.

verb   *un verbe* = a "doing" or "being" word
Je **parle** anglais. Il **est** blond. On **va** en ville. Nous **faisons** du sport.

tense   *le temps* = tells you when an action takes place

adjective   *un adjectif* = a word which describes a noun
Ton frère est **sympa**.
C'est un appartement **moderne**.

preposition   *une préposition* = often describes position: where something is
Mon sac est **sur** mon lit. J'habite **à** Paris.

1 Nouns and determiners

les noms et les déterminants

1.1 Masculine or feminine?

All French nouns are either masculine or feminine.
Determiners must match.

	masculine words	feminine words
a or *an*	un	une
the	le	la

un *sport*, **le** *taxi* = masculine
une *question*, **la** *maison* = feminine

Important! When you meet a new noun, learn whether it is masculine or feminine.

learn	*un café*	✔
not	*café*	✗

1.2 Singular or plural?

Most French nouns add –s to make them plural, just as in English:

> *la jambe* ⟶ *les jambes*

(In French the *–s* at the end of the word is not usually pronounced.)

Exceptions:
- nouns already ending in *–s*, *–x* or *–z* usually stay the same:
  le bras ⟶ *les bras*
  le prix ⟶ *les prix*
- nouns ending in *-eau* or *-eu* add *-x*:
  un chapeau ⟶ *des chapeaux*
  un jeu ⟶ *des jeux*
- nouns ending in *-al* usually change to *-aux*:
  un animal ⟶ *des animaux*
- a few nouns change completely:
  un œil ⟶ *des yeux*

In front of plural nouns, the determiners change:
> *un/une* ⟶ *des*
> *le/la* ⟶ *les*

*Je mange **une** banane.*	I'm eating a banana.
*Je mange **des** bananes.*	I'm eating bananas.
***Le** match a commencé.*	The match has started.
***Les** matchs ont commencé.*	The matches have started.

1.3 de + noun = *some / any*

	singular	plural
masculine words	du (*or* de l')	des
feminine words	de la (*or* de l')	des

Use *du, de la, de l'* or *des* + noun to say some or any.
> *On a mangé **des** croissants avec **de la** confiture.*
> We ate **some** croissants with jam.
> *Tu as **du** chocolat?*
> Have you got **any** chocolate?

1.4 Talking about jobs

As in English, some jobs are the same whether the person is a man or a woman:
un médecin a doctor
un/une journaliste a journalist

More often, the French names of jobs are different for men and women:

	masculine	feminine
a hairdresser	*un coiffeur*	*une coiffeuse*
a youth worker	*un éducateur*	*une éducatrice*
a mechanic	*un mécanicien*	*une mécanicienne*
a lawyer	*un avocat*	*une avocate*

Saying what job someone does is one of the few times a noun in French does not have *le/la/les* or *un/une/des* in front of it:
> *Je voudrais être dentiste.*
> I'd like to be **a** dentist.

Grammaire

2 Adjectives

les adjectifs

2.1 Form of adjectives

In English, whatever you are describing, the adjective stays exactly the same. In French, the adjective changes to match the word it is describing. Like the noun, it must be either masculine or feminine, singular or plural.

To show this, there are special adjective endings:

	singular	plural
masculine words	add nothing	add –s
feminine words	add –e	add –es

mon père est petit *mes frères sont petit**s***
*ma mère est petit**e*** *mes sœurs sont petit**es***

Exceptions:
- Adjectives that end in –e don't add another in the feminine (but they do add –s in the plural):
  un frère calme ⟶ *une sœur calme*
  *des enfants calm**es***
- Adjectives ending in –eur or –eux usually change to –euse in the feminine:
  un frère travailleur ⟶ *une sœur travaill**euse***
  un frère courageux ⟶ *une sœur courag**euse***
- A very few adjectives stay the same whether they are masculine or feminine, singular or plural:
  un cousin sympa
  une cousine sympa
  des cousins sympa
  le foot est super
  la France est super
  les films sont super

- Some adjectives have their own pattern: ·

singular		plural	
masculine	**feminine**	**masc./mixed**	**feminine**
blanc	blanche	blancs	blanches
bon	bonne	bons	bonnes
gros	grosse	gros	grosses
violet	violette	violets	violettes
beau*	belle	beaux	belles
nouveau*	nouvelle	nouveaux	nouvelles
vieux*	vieille	vieux	vieilles

* become *bel*, *nouvel*, *vieil* before a masculine noun that starts with a vowel, e.g. *le nouvel an*

2.2 Position of adjectives

In English, **adjectives** always come before the noun they describe:
a **great** <u>film</u>, a **modern** <u>kitchen</u>, **nice** <u>friends</u>.

In French, **adjectives** usually come after the noun:
*un <u>film</u> **génial**, une **cuisine** <u>moderne</u>, des <u>copains</u> **sympa**.*

Some adjectives break this rule of position. The following come before the noun:

grand	*petit*	*gros*
nouveau	*jeune*	*vieux*
beau	*bon*	*mauvais*

*un **nouveau** portable*   *la **jeune** fille*   *de **bonnes** idées*

 Write out the sentences adding the adjectives in brackets in the right position.

Example *J'ai une maison.* [petite, moderne] ⟶
J'ai une petite maison moderne.

a On a vu un film. [français]

b J'ai acheté deux T-shirts. [noirs]

c J'aime bien le chanteur. [jeune]

d Tu vois la porte à gauche? [petite]

e Il y a un cinéma. [moderne]

f On a mangé un repas. [délicieux]

g Elle a une robe. [blanche, belle]

h Mon frère a un portable. [nouveau, bleu]

i Ils ont regardé une émission. [intéressante, nouvelle]

2.3 The comparative

To compare, use *plus*, *moins* or *aussi*:

plus + adjective/adverb + *que*	more ... than
moins + adjective/adverb + *que*	less ... than
aussi + adjective/adverb + *que*	as ... as

– with an adjective:

*Le livre est **plus intéressant que** le film.*
The book is **more interesting than** the film.

*L'appartement est **moins cher que** la maison.*
The flat is **less expensive than** the house.

*Elle est **aussi grande que** moi.*
She's **as tall as** me.

 Bon (good) and *mauvais* (bad) are exceptions:

bon ⟶ *meilleur*

*Le film est **meilleur que** le livre.*
The film is **better than** the book.

mauvais ⟶ *pire*

*Le livre est **pire que** le film.*
The book is **worse than** the film.

3 The possessive
la possession

3.1 The possessive of nouns

To show who (or what) things belong to, use *de* (of) with nouns:

*les baskets **de Natacha***	**Natacha's** trainers
*les questions **des élèves***	**the pupils'** questions

 B Translate into French.

Example Bruno's bedroom = *la chambre de Bruno*

a Samira's brothers

b the teacher's book

c the children's ideas

d the old lady's cat

e Dad's computer

3.2 Possessive adjectives

These adjectives show who or what something belongs to (**my** bag, **your** CD, **his** brother).

They come before the noun they describe, in place of *un/une/des* or *le/la/les*, for example.

Like all adjectives, they have to match the noun they describe:

	singular		plural
	masculine	**feminine***	**masculine or feminine**
my	mon	ma	mes
your	ton	ta	tes
his/her	son	sa	ses
our	notre	notre	nos
your	votre	votre	vos
their	leur	leur	leurs

*Before a feminine noun that begins with a vowel, use *mon, ton, son* (*mon imagination, ton amie, son opinion*).

 The words for *his* and *her* are the same (either *son, sa* or *ses*, depending on the word that follows).

*Karima adore **son** chien.*   Karima loves **her** dog.
*Marc adore **son** chien.*   Marc loves **his** dog.

C Translate into French using the correct possessive adjectives.

a It's my magazine.

b Your CD is in her bedroom.

c His mobile is in my bag.

d His cousins don't like their teacher.

e Their mother is a doctor and their father is a dentist.

f Their house is bigger than our house.

g My girlfriend bought your tickets.

h She went with her mother and her father.

i Put your jacket in my wardrobe.

j Do you like our dog and our cats?

k My grandparents are Italian. I love their pizzas!

l Where are your pen and your pencils?

Grammaire

4 Prepositions
les prépositions

The prepositions below describe position:

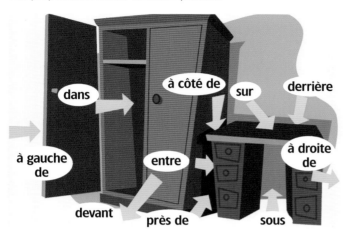

dans · à côté de · sur · derrière · à gauche de · entre · à droite de · devant · près de · sous

4.1 à (at, in, to)

- *à* combines with *le* or *les* in front of the noun to form a completely new word:

  à + le ⟶ *au*
  à + les ⟶ *aux* } *= to / at the*

	singular	**plural**
masculine words	au (*or* à l')	aux
feminine words	à la (*or* à l')	aux

- Time
  Use *à* to say *at* a time:
  *J'ai français **à** quatre heures.*   I have French **at** four o'clock.

- Places
  Use *à* to say *at, in* or *to* a place, combining it with the determiner in masculine or plural:
  *J'habite **à** Paris.*   I live **in** Paris.
  *Je vais **à la** gare.*   I am going **to the** station.
  *Il est **au** cinéma.*   He's **at the** cinema.

> **Choose *à, à la* or *au* to complete the sentences.**
> **a** Cet avion va [à / à la / au] Manchester.
> **b** Tu veux rentrer [à / à la / au] maison?
> **c** Vous allez [à / à la / au] café?
> **d** Je ne vais pas [à / à la / au] collège le samedi.

* To say *there*, use the pronoun *y*. See section 5.4.

- Parts of the body that hurt
  Use *à* in front of the part of the body, combining it with the determiner in masculine or plural:
  *J'ai mal **à la** tête.*   I've got a headache.
  *Max a mal **au** dos.*   Max has backache.
  *Tu as mal **aux** dents?*   Have you got toothache?

4.2 en (in, to, by)

- Places
  In French, most names of countries are feminine. To say *in* or *to* these countries, use the word *en*:
  *Vous allez **en** France?*   Are you going **to** France?
  *J'habite **en** Écosse.*   I live **in** Scotland.

⚠ For masculine names of countries, use *au*, and *aux* for plural names (see 4.1).
  *Cardiff est **au** pays de Galles.*
  Cardiff is **in** Wales.
  *Ma cousine va **aux** États-Unis.*
  My cousin's going **to the** United States.

  en ville = in or to town

- Time
  ***en** juin*   **in** June
  ***en** hiver*   **in** winter
  ***en** 2012*   **in** 2012

- Means of transport
  Use *en* + name of means of transport to say how you travel:
  ***en** train*   **by** train
  ***en** bus*   **by** bus
  ***en** voiture*   **by** car
  ***en** avion*   **by** plane

⚠ For walking or a two-wheeled vehicle, use *à* + means of transport (without a determiner):
  *Il va **à** pied.*   He is walking.
  *Elle va **à** vélo.*   She is going **by** bike.
  *Nous allons **à** mobylette.*   We are going **by** moped.

5 Pronouns

les pronoms

A pronoun is used instead of a noun or name to avoid repetition.

My cat is called Tigger. Tigger sleeps in a box.

= **He** sleeps in a box.

5.1 Subject pronouns

The subject of a verb tells you who or what is doing the action of the verb. It is usually a noun, but sometimes it is a pronoun. In English, we use the following subject pronouns:

I you he she it we they

I'm learning French. Are **you**?

Annie is learning Italian. **She** loves it.

The French subject pronouns are:

| I | = | je | |
| | | j' | in front of a vowel or a silent *h*: *j'aime/j'habite* |

| you | = | tu | when talking to a child, a friend or a relative |
| | | vous | when talking to an adult you are not related to, or more than one person |

| he | = | *il* | for a boy or man |

| she | = | *elle* | for a girl or woman |

| it | = | *il* | if the noun it refers to is masculine |
| | | *elle* | if the noun it refers to is feminine |

| we | = | *nous* | |
| | | *on* | used more than *nous* in conversation. |

Use *on* when speaking or writing to friends.
Use *nous* when writing more "official" texts.

they =		*ils*	for a masculine plural or for a mixed group (masculine + feminine)
		elles	for a feminine plural
		on	when it means people in general

On

On can mean you, we, they or one.

It is followed by the form of the verb that follows *il* or *elle*:

*Chez moi, **on parle** arabe.*

At home **we speak** Arabic.

5.6 Emphatic pronouns

The French emphatic pronouns are:

moi	me, I	**nous**	us, we
toi	you	**vous**	you
lui	him, he	**eux**	them, they (masculine)
elle	her, she	**elles**	them, they (feminine)

Use an emphatic pronoun:

- to emphasize a subject pronoun (in English we usually put more emphasis on the pronoun rather than add a word):

  ***Moi**, je fais mon stage à l'office du tourisme.*

  *Et **toi**, tu vas où?*

  I'm doing my work placement at the tourist office. What about you? Where are **you** going?

6 Verbs

les verbes

Verbs describe what is happening. If you can put *to* in front of a word or *-ing* at the end, it is probably a verb.*

listen − to listen ✓ = a verb

try − to try ✓ = verb

desk − to desk ✗ = not a verb

happy − to happy ✗ = not a verb

* Some words can be nouns as well as verbs, such as *to drink* (verb) and *a drink* (noun).

6.1 The infinitive

Infinitives in French are easy to recognize as they normally end with either *-er*, *-re* or *-ir*. For example: *regarder, prendre, choisir*.

Grammaire

6.2 The present tense

A verb in the present tense describes an action which is taking place now or takes place regularly.

> Je **vais** au collège maintenant. (now)
> Je **vais** au collège tous les jours. (every day)

● Regular verbs in the present tense

Most French verbs follow the same pattern. They have regular endings.

Typical endings for verbs that end in *-er*, like *aimer* (to like), in the present tense are:

j'	aim**e**	nous	aim**ons**
tu	aim**es**	vous	aim**ez**
il/elle/on	aim**e**	ils/elles	aim**ent**

Some other verbs which follow the same pattern are: *adorer (to love), arriver (to arrive), détester (to hate), écouter (to listen), jouer (to play), parler (to speak), regarder (to watch / look).*

Typical endings for verbs that end in *-ir*, like *choisir* (to choose), in the present tense are:

je	chois**is**	nous	chois**issons**
tu	chois**is**	vous	chois**issez**
il/elle/on	chois**it**	ils/elles	chois**issent**

Some other verbs which follow the same pattern are: *finir (to finish), remplir (to fill).*

Typical endings for verbs that end in *-re*, like *vendre* (to sell), in the present tense are:

je	vend**s**	nous	vend**ons**
tu	vend**s**	vous	vend**ez**
il/elle/on	vend	ils/elles	vend**ent**

Some other verbs which follow the same pattern are: *attendre (to wait), descendre (to go down), perdre (to lose), répondre (to respond).*

● Irregular verbs in the present tense

Some verbs do not follow this regular pattern. They are irregular verbs. Find the present tense forms of these useful verbs in the verb tables on pages 141–142 and try to learn them by heart, particularly the ones in bold print:

aller (to go) *avoir* (to have) *devoir* (to have to)
être (to be) *faire* (to do) *mettre* (to put)
pouvoir (to be able to) *prendre* (to take) *sortir* (to go out)
venir (to come) *voir* (to see) *vouloir* (to want to)

 E Change the infinitives in brackets to the correct form of the present tense verb.

a Je [aller] en ville.

b Je [devoir] faire la vaisselle.

c C' [être] l'anniversaire de ma mère.

d Tu [faire] souvent la cuisine?

e Tu [pouvoir] venir avec moi?

f Ma copine [venir] chez nous et nous [boire] du thé.

g On [prendre] le bus qui [partir] à neuf heures.

h Il [aller] au cinéma mais je [regarder] la télé.

i Je [sortir] avec le garçon qui [avoir] le jean noir.

j Le matin, il [prendre] le train et il [lire] le journal.

6.3 The perfect tense

A verb in the perfect tense (*passé composé*) describes an action which happened in the past. There are several ways to translate the *passé composé* in English:

***J'ai regardé** la télé.*
I watched TV. or **I have watched** TV.

For the *passé composé*, you need two parts: the present tense of *avoir* or *être* + the past participle of the main verb. See 6.4, 6.5 and 6.6.

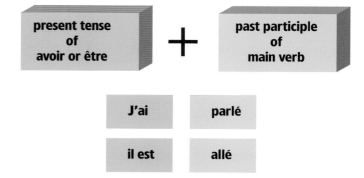

6.4 The past participle

To form the past participle, take the infinitive of the verb and change the ending:

- infinitives ending in *-er*: past participle ends in *-é*
  manger ⟶ *mangé* (eaten)
  parler ⟶ *parlé* (spoken)
- infinitives ending in *-ir*: past participle ends in *-i*
  choisir ⟶ *choisi* (chosen)
  sortir ⟶ *sorti* (gone out)
- infinitives ending in *-re*: past participle ends in *-u*
  descendre ⟶ *descendu* (gone down)
  vendre ⟶ *vendu* (sold)

There are some exceptions to the above rules. Check the verb tables on pages 141–142 to find them. Learn by heart these common exceptions:

avoir ⟶ *eu* (had)	*être* ⟶ *été* (been)
faire ⟶ *fait* (done)	*voir* ⟶ *vu* (seen)
boire ⟶ *bu* (drunk)	*venir* ⟶ *venu* (come)
mettre ⟶ *mis* (put)	*prendre* ⟶ *pris* (taken)
pouvoir ⟶ *pu* (been able)	*vouloir* ⟶ *voulu* (wanted)

 Copy and complete the sentences with the correct past participles.

1 J'ai [**fait / faire**] un échange avec Jade Smith en Angleterre.
2 J'ai [**prendre / pris**] le train et le bateau.
3 Pendant le voyage, j'ai [**mangé / mange**] un sandwich et j'ai [**lis / lu**] un livre intéressant.
4 J'ai bien [**aimer / aimé**] les repas chez les Smith.
5 Avec le repas du soir, on a [**bu / bois**] du lait – bizarre!
6 On a [**visité / visiter**] Londres deux fois et on a [**regarde / regardé**] un match de cricket à Woking.
7 On ne joue pas au cricket en France et c'est la première fois que j'ai [**vu / voit**] un match.
8 J'ai [**peux / pu**] beaucoup parler anglais et j'ai [**fait / fais**] beaucoup de progrès!

6.5 avoir + past participle

Most verbs form the perfect tense with part of *avoir*:

présent	*passé composé*		
		avoir	**past participle**
I watched	j'	ai	regardé
You watched	tu	as	regardé
He watched	il	a	regardé
She watched	elle	a	regardé
We watched	on	a	regardé
We watched	nous	avons	regardé
You watched	vous	avez	regardé
They watched	ils	ont	regardé
They watched	elles	ont	regardé

6.6 être + past participle

Some verbs form the perfect tense with *être*, not *avoir*.

	passé composé		
		être	**past participle**
I arrived	je	suis	arrivé(e)
you arrived	tu	es	arrivé(e)
he arrived	il	est	arrivé
she arrived	elle	est	arrivée
we arrived	on	est	arrivés
we arrived	nous	sommes	arrivé(e)s
you arrived	vous	êtes	arrivé(e)(s)
they arrived	ils	sont	arrivés
they arrived	elles	sont	arrivées

These are mostly verbs that indicate movement from one place to another. You will need to learn by heart which they are.

Try learning them in pairs:

arriver / partir	to arrive / to leave
aller / venir	to go / to come
entrer / sortir	to go in / to go out
monter / descendre	to go up / to go down
rentrer / retourner	to go home / to go back
tomber / rester	to fall / to stay
naître / mourir	to be born / to die

Grammaire

- The ending of the past participle changes when it comes after *être* in the *passé composé*. It agrees with the subject of the verb (masculine / feminine, singular / plural).

Je suis allé en France.
(Il est allé en France.)

Je suis allée en France.
(Elle est allée en France.)

G **Copy and complete with perfect tense verbs. Be sure to check that the past participle agrees with the subject of the verb.**

Example *Laura [partir] ce matin.* ⟶ Laura est partie ce matin.

a Papa [arriver] à six heures.
b Ma tante [monter] à la tour Eiffel.
c Laura [aller] au cinéma.
d Jérémy [aller] au bowling.
e David [rester] à la maison.
f On [descendre] dans le métro.
g Le prof [entrer] dans la salle de classe.
h Julie [sortir] avec mon cousin.
i Ma mère [naître] dans le sud de la France.
j Marie-Antoinette [mourir] lors de la Révolution française.

6.7 The imperfect tense

The imperfect tense is used in two different ways in *Clic! 3*:

- To describe a person or thing in the past, using *être*:

C'était génial!	It **was** great!
J'étais content(e).	I **was** happy.
Les profs étaient sympa.	The teachers **were** nice.

- To describe an action which used to happen or which happened often in the past:

J'écoutais des histoires.	I **used to listen to** stories.
On **allait** au bord de la mer.	We **used to go** to the seaside.

Then add the correct ending according to who is doing the action of the verb:

faire			
je	fais**ais**	nous	fais**ions**
tu	fais**ais**	vous	fais**iez**
il/elle/on	fais**ait**	ils/elles	fais**aient**

Use the verb tables on pages 141–142 to check the imperfect forms of some common verbs.

⚠ There is only one exception to the rule for forming the imperfect: the verb *être*. It uses the same endings, but on the stem *ét-*: *j'étais*, etc.

H **Copy out the text using the right form of imperfect tense verbs.**

1 Le week-end, quand j' [**étais** / **était**] petit, je [**regardais** / **regardait**] la télé.
2 Je [**jouait** / **jouais**] aussi au football avec mes frères.
3 On [**aimait** / **aimais**] beaucoup ça!
4 Le week-end, mes parents [**était** / **étaient**] toujours fatigués.
5 Papa [**dormais** / **dormait**] jusqu'à midi et Maman [**lisaient** / **lisait**] des magazines dans le séjour.
6 C'[**étais** / **était**] toujours calme chez nous!
7 De temps en temps, on [**allait** / **allais**] en ville.
8 On [**visitais** / **visitait**] un musée ou une galerie d'art.
9 Je [**détestaient** / **détestais**] ces sorties.
10 Il n'y [**avait** / **avais**] rien à faire pour les enfants.

6.8 Perfect or imperfect?

How do you know which past tense to use?

- Use the perfect to talk about one particular event in the past:
  Je suis allée au centre de vacances.
  I **went** to the holiday camp.
  J'ai pris le train.
  I **took** the train.

- Use the imperfect if you are describing what something was like or talking about what used to happen:

*La fête **était** super.*

The party **was** great.

*À l'école primaire, je **jouais** avec mes copains.*

At primary school, I **used to play** with my friends.

> **Choose the perfect or the imperfect.**
> a Samedi dernier, on **a mangé / mangeait** dans une crêperie.
> b À l'école primaire, on **a chanté / chantait** tous les jours.
> c Dans les années 50, on **a écouté / écoutait** souvent la radio.
> d En 2008, nous **avons passé / passions** un week-end au bord de la mer à Dinard.
> e Quand **j'ai été / j'étais** petit, **je suis allé / j'allais** chez mon père tous les week-ends.

6.9 depuis + present tense

Depuis can usually be translated as 'since' or 'for'. Use it to talk about *what has been and still is* going on. In English the verb stresses the past, but in French, the verb stresses the present:

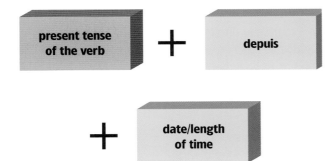

J'habite au Canada depuis 2007.
I have been living in Canada since 2007 (and I still do).
On joue au basket depuis deux ans.
We have been playing basketball for two years.

6.10 Talking about the future

- To talk about something that is going to happen in the near future:

  – Use the present tense with a time indicator, as in English:

  Je fais mes devoirs demain.
  I'm doing my homework tomorrow.
  Il part ce soir.
  He leaves this evening.

– Use the present tense of the verb *aller* + infinitive:

present tense of aller	+	infinitive of main verb

*Tu **vas travailler** ce week-end?*
Are you going to work this weekend?
*Oui, je **vais travailler** samedi.*
Yes, I am going to work on Saturday.

- There is also a special future tense to talk about what someone will do or what will happen.
  The future tense is formed by adding the following endings to the infinitive form of the verb:*

je	regarder**ai**	nous	regarder**ons**
tu	regarder**as**	vous	regarder**ez**
il/elle/on	regarder**a**	ils/elles	regarder**ont**

There are some exceptions to this rule, where the stem is not the infinitive, e.g. *être − ser-* , *avoir − aur-*, *faire − fer-*. See the verb tables on pages 141–142.

- If you are talking about future plans which are not certain (wishes, ambitions or dreams), use *je/tu voudrais* + infinitive:
  *Je **voudrais être** chanteur.*
  I **would like to be** a singer.
  *Tu **voudrais habiter** en France?*
  Would you **like** to **live** in France?

6.11 Reflexive verbs

Reflexive verbs need a pronoun between the subject and the verb.

subject	pronoun	verb	
↓	↓	↓	
Je	**me**	lève	(I get myself up) I get up.
Je	**m'**	habille	(I dress myself) I get dressed.

Some common reflexive verbs: *se laver (to wash), se brosser les dents (to brush one's teeth), se réveiller (to wake up), s'amuser (to have fun), s'ennuyer (to be bored), se coucher (to go to bed), se reposer (to rest)*

Grammaire

The pronoun changes according to the subject it goes with:

je	+ **me** / **m'**	nous	+ **nous**
tu	+ **te** / **t'**	vous	+ **vous**
il / elle / on	+ **se** / **s'**	ils / elles	+ **se** / **s'**

All reflexive verbs make their perfect tense with *être*. The reflexive pronoun goes in front of the part of *être*:

Je me **suis** *brossé les dents.* I brushed my teeth.

The past participle agrees with the subject in gender and in number:

*Anne s'est couch**ée** de bonne heure.*
Anne went to bed early.

6.12 The imperative

The imperative is the form of the verb you use to give someone an order, an instruction or advice:
Eat! Go to bed. Turn left.

When giving an instruction to:
- someone you say *tu* to:
  use the *tu* form of the verb.

- someone you say *vous* to (or more than one person):
  use the *vous* form of the verb.

	tu	*vous*
Eat!	*Mange!*	*Mangez!*
Turn left!	*Tourne à gauche!*	*Tournez à gauche!*
Do some sport!	*Fais du sport!*	*Faites du sport!*
Go to bed.	*Va au lit.*	*Allez au lit.*
Save water.	*Économise l'eau.*	*Économisez l'eau.*

6.13 Verb + infinitive

Sometimes there are two verbs next to each other in a sentence. The form of **the first verb depends on the subject**, and the second verb is in the infinitive.

J'aime <u>aller</u> au cinéma.	I like going to the cinema.
Tu dois <u>faire</u> tes devoirs.	You must do your homework.
On préfère <u>lire</u> ce livre.	We prefer to read this book.
Il va <u>manger</u> du pain.	He's going to eat some bread.

- *aller* + infinitive – talking about the future
  Use the present tense of the verb *aller* followed by an infinitive to talk about something that is going to happen in the near future (see 6.10):
  Je vais retrouver *Juliette à six heures.*
  I'm going to meet Juliette at six o'clock.
  Ils vont manger au *restaurant ce soir.*
  They are going to eat at the restaurant this evening.

- *devoir, pouvoir, vouloir*
  These verbs are nearly always followed by the infinitive of another verb.
  devoir – to have to (I must)
  > *Elle* **doit** <u>se coucher</u>.
  > She **has to** go to bed.
  > *Vous* **devez** <u>manger</u> des légumes.
  > You **must** eat vegetables.

  pouvoir – to be able to (I can)
  > *On* **peut** <u>se retrouver</u> demain?
  > Can we **meet** tomorrow?
  > *Je* **peux** <u>m'habiller</u> comme je veux.
  > I **can** dress how I like.

  vouloir – to want
  > *Tu* **veux** <u>rester</u> à la maison?
  > **Do** you **want** to stay at home?
  > *Ils* **veulent** <u>sortir</u>.
  > They **want** to go out.

See the full pattern of the present tense of these verbs on pages 141–142.

The infinitive is also used after *il faut* and *il ne faut pas*:
> **Il faut** <u>faire</u> tes devoirs.
> **You have to** do your homework.
> **Il ne faut pas** attendre.
> **You don't have to** wait.

6.14 jouer à / jouer de

To talk about playing games or sport, use *jouer **à***:
*J'aime jouer **au** football.*   I like playing football.

To talk about playing a musical instrument, use *jouer **de***:
*Je joue **de la** guitare.*   I play the guitar.

Remember:
à + le = **au**   de + le = **du**
à + les = **aux**   de + les = **des**

7   Negatives
la négation

In English, the most common negative form uses the word *not*
or *–n't* as in *doesn't, don't, haven't, hasn't*.

In French, use ***ne*** and ***pas***, which go on either side of the verb
(*ne* = *n'* in front of a vowel or a silent *h*):
*Je **ne** suis **pas** français.*   I'm **not** French.
*Elle **n'a pas** de sandales.*   She has**n't** got any sandals.
*On **ne** regarde **pas** la télé.*   We do**n't** watch TV.

 Complete the answers.

a Tu parles japonais? Non, je…

b Samuel aime les hamsters? Non, il …

c Karima sortait avec Max? Non, elle …

d Tes parents sont contents? Non, ils …

e On va à la piscine? Non, on…

7.1   ne… jamais, ne… rien, ne… plus

Some other negatives which also go on either side of the verb:
ne (or *n'*) … *jamais*	never
ne (or *n'*) … *rien*	nothing/not anything
ne (or *n'*) … *plus*	no longer, no more

*Je **ne** vais **jamais** au cinéma.*
I **never** go to the cinema.
*Elle **ne** mange **rien**.*
She doesn**'t** eat **anything**.
*Ils **n'**habitent **plus** en France.*
They **no longer** live in France.

7.2 Negative + de / d' + noun

If you use *ne … pas / jamais / plus* with a noun, replace
un / une / des before the noun with *de* (or *d'* in front of a
vowel or a silent *h*):

*Il **n'**y a **pas de** pizza / fromage / chips.*
There is**n't any** pizza / cheese / there are**n't any** crisps.
*On **n'a plus de** chocolat.*
We have**n't** got **any more** chocolate.
*Je **n'**ai **jamais d'**argent.*
I **never** have **any** money.

Grammaire

Answers

A
a On a vu un film français.
b J'ai acheté deux T-shirts noirs.
c J'aime bien le jeune chanteur.
d Tu vois la petite porte à gauche?
e Il y a un cinéma moderne.
f On a mangé un repas délicieux.
g Elle a une belle robe blanche.
h Mon frère a un nouveau portable bleu.
i Ils ont regardé une nouvelle émission intéressante.

B
a les frères de Samira
b le livre du prof(esseur)
c les idées des enfants
d le chat de la vieille dame
e l'ordinateur de Papa

C
a C'est mon magazine.
b Ton (or Votre) CD est dans sa chambre.
c Son portable est dans mon sac.
d Ses cousins n'aiment pas leur prof(esseur).
e Leur mère est médecin et leur père est dentiste.
f Leur maison est plus grande que notre maison.
g Ma copine a acheté tes (or vos) billets.
h Elle est allée avec sa mère et son père.
i Mets (or Mettez) ta (or votre) veste dans mon armoire.
j Tu aimes (or Vous aimez) notre chien et nos chats?
k Mes grands-parents sont italiens. J'adore leurs pizzas!
l Où sont ton (or votre) stylo et tes (or vos) crayons?

D
a à
b à la
c au
d au

E
a vais
b dois
c est
d fais
e peux
f vient, buvons
g prend, part
h va, regarde
i sors, a
j prend, lit

F
1 fait **2** pris **3** mange **4** lu **5** aime **6** bu **7** visite
8 regarde **9** vu **10** pu **11** fait

G
a est arrivé
b est montée
c est allée
d est allé
e est resté
f est descendu
g est entré
h est sortie
i est née
j est morte

H
1 étais **2** regardais **3** jouais **4** aimait **5** étaient
6 dormait **7** lisait **8** était **9** allait **10** visitait
11 détestais **12** avait

I
a on a mangé
b on chantait
c on écoutait
d nous avons passé
e j'étais, je suis allé

J
a Non, je ne parle pas japonais.
b Non, il n'aime pas les hamsters.
c Non, elle sortait pas avec Max.
d Non, ils ne sont pas contents.
e Non, on ne va pas à la piscine.

8 Verb tables

infinitive	present		perfect	imperfect	future
–er verbs PARLER (to speak)	je parle tu parles il/elle/on parle	nous parlons vous parlez ils/elles parlent	j'ai parlé	je parlais	je parlerai
–ir verbs FINIR (to finish)	je finis tu finis il/elle/on finit	nous finissons vous finissez ils/elles finissent	j'ai fini	je finissais	je finirai
–re verbs VENDRE (to sell)	je vends tu vends il/elle/on vend	nous vendons vous vendez ils/elles vendent	j'ai vendu	je vendais	je vendrai
reflexive verbs SE COUCHER (to go to bed)	je me couche tu te couches il/elle/on se couche	nous nous couchons vous vous couchez ils/elles se couchent	je me suis couché(e)	je me couchais	je me coucherai
irregular verbs ALLER (to go)	je vais tu vas il/elle/on va	nous allons vous allez ils/elles vont	je suis allé(e)	j'allais	j'irai
AVOIR (to have)	j'ai tu as il a	nous avons vous avez ils ont	j'ai eu	j'avais	j'aurai
BOIRE (to drink)	je bois tu bois il/elle/on boit	nous buvons vous buvez ils/elles boivent	j'ai bu	je buvais	je boirai
DEVOIR (to have to)	je dois tu dois il/elle/on doit	nous devons vous devez ils/elles doivent	j'ai dû	je devais	je devrai
DIRE (to say)	je dis tu dis il/elle/on dit	nous disons vous dites ils/elles disent	j'ai dit	je disais	je dirai
DORMIR (to sleep)	je dors tu dors il/elle/on dort	nous dormons vous dormez ils/elles dorment	j'ai dormi	je dormais	je dormirai
ÉCRIRE (to write)	j'écris tu écris il/elle/on écrit	nous écrivons vous écrivez ils/elles écrivent	j'ai écrit	j'écrivais	j'écrirai
ÊTRE (to be)	je suis tu es il/elle/on est	nous sommes vous êtes ils/elles sont	j'ai été	j'étais	je serai

Grammaire

infinitive	present		perfect	imperfect	future
FAIRE (to do/make)	je fais tu fais il/elle/on fait	nous faisons vous faites ils/elles font	j'ai fait	je faisais	je ferai
LIRE (to read)	je lis tu lis il/elle/on lit	nous lisons vous lisez ils/elles lisent	j'ai lu	je lisais	je lirai
METTRE (to put/put on)	je mets tu mets il/elle/on met	nous mettons vous mettez ils/elles mettent	j'ai mis	je mettais	je mettrai
POUVOIR (to be able to)	je peux tu peux il/elle/on peut	nous pouvons vous pouvez ils/elles peuvent	j'ai pu	je pouvais	je pourrai
PRENDRE (to take)	je prends tu prends il/elle/on prend	nous prenons vous prenez ils/elles prennent	j'ai pris	je prenais	je prendrai
SAVOIR (to know)	je sais tu sais il/elle/on sait	nous savons vous savez ils/elles savent	j'ai su	je savais	je saurai
SORTIR (to go out)	je sors tu sors il/elle/on sort	nous sortons vous sortez ils/elles sortent	je suis sorti(e)	je sortais	je sortirai
VENIR (to come)	je viens tu viens il/elle/on vient	nous venons vous venez ils/elles viennent	je suis venu(e)	je venais	je viendrai
VOIR (to see)	je vois tu vois il/elle/on voit	nous voyons vous voyez ils/elles voient	j'ai vu	je voyais	je verrai
VOULOIR (to want)	je veux tu veux il/elle/on veut	nous voulons vous voulez ils/elles veulent	j'ai voulu	je voulais	je voudrai

il/elle/on **a** he/she/it has, we have
à at, in, to
une **abeille** *nf* a bee
d' **abord** first
acheter *v* to buy
d' **accord** OK
un **acteur** *nm* an actor (male)
une **activité** *nf* an activity
une **actrice** *nf* an actress
additionner *v* to add up
un **adjectif** *nm* an adjective
un **adolescent** *nm* a teenager
adorer *v* to love
une **adresse** *nf* an address
s' **adresser** *v* to apply
un **adulte** *nm* an adult
un **aéroport** *nm* an airport
des **affaires** *nf pl* things, belongings
une **affiche** *nf* a poster
afficher *v* to stick up
affreux/affreuse *adj* terrible
l' **Afrique** *nf* Africa
l' **âge** *nm* age
un **agent de police** *nm* a police officer
agréable *adj* pleasant
j' **ai** I have
aider *v* to help
aimer *v* to like, to love
ajouter *v* to add
a l'air... (he/she) looks...
l' **Algérie** *nf* Algeria
algérien/algérienne *adj* Algerian
un **aliment** *nm* a foodstuff
l' **Allemagne** *nf* Germany
allemand/allemande *adj* German
aller *v* to go
vous **allez** you go
allô hello (over the phone)
nous **allons** we go
alors so, then
l' **alpinisme** *nm* mountaineering
l' **ambiance** *nf* atmosphere
améliorer *v* to improve
américain/américaine *adj* American
un **ami** *nm* a friend (male)
une **amie** *nf* a friend (female)
l' **amitié** *nf* friendship
amitiés best wishes (in a letter)
amusant/amusante *adj* funny, amusing
un **an** *nm* a year
l' **ananas** *nm* pineapple
ancien/ancienne *adj* old
à ne pas manquer not to be missed

anglais/anglaise *adj* English
l' **Angleterre** *nf* England
un **animal** *nm* animal
un/une **animateur/animatrice** *nm/f* an activity leader (in a holiday camp)
une **année** *nf* a year
un **anniversaire** *nm* a birthday
une **annonce** *nf* an advert
août August
un **appareil dentaire** *nm* braces
un **appareil photo numérique** *nm* a digital camera
un mot **apparenté** *nm* a cognate
un **appartement** *nm* a flat
s' **appeler** *v* to be called
je m' **appelle...** my name is...
tu t' **appelles...** your name is...
il/elle **s'appelle** his/her name is...
apprendre *v* to learn
approprié/appropriée *adj* appropriate
après after
l' **après-midi** *nm* the afternoon
l' **arabe** *nm* Arabic
l' **arbitre** *nm* referee
l' **argent** *nm* money
une **armoire** *nf* a wardrobe
arrêter *v* to stop
l' **arrivée** *nf* finish line
arriver *v* to arrive
tu **as** you have
assez rather, enough
assister *v* to watch (a match), to go to
l' **athlétisme** *nm* athletics
à tout à l'heure see you later
attendre *v* to wait
une **auberge de jeunesse** *nf* a youth hostel
aucun/aucune *adj* no, none
aujourd'hui today
auprès de according to
aussi too
l' **Australie** *nf* Australia
l' **automne** *nm* autumn
un **automobiliste** *nm* a driver
l' **autre** *nm* other
d' **avance** in advance
avancer *v* to go forward
avant before
avec with
vous **avez** you have
un **avion** *nm* a plane
un **avis** *nm* an opinion
à mon **avis** in my opinion
avoir *v* to have
nous **avons** we have
avril April

le **baby-foot** *nm* table football
une **baguette** *nf* a French loaf
la **baignade** *nf* swimming
un **bain** *nm* a bath
baisser *v* to lower
un **baladeur (MP3)** *nm* an MP3 player/walkman
le **balcon** *nm* balcony
un **ballon de foot** *nm* a football
une **banane** *nf* a banana
une **bande dessinée** *nf* a cartoon
la **banlieue** *nf* the suburbs
en **banlieue parisienne** in the Paris suburbs
un **barbecue** *nm* a barbecue
un/une **basketteur/basketteuse** *nm/f* a basketball player
un **bateau** *nm* a boat
un **bâtiment** *nm* **a** building
un **bâton de colle** *nm* a glue-stick
bavard/bavarde *adj* talkative
beau/belle *adj* beautiful
un **beau-père** *nm* a step-father
beaucoup a lot
un **bébé** *nm* a baby
belge *adj* Belgian
la **Belgique** *nf* Belgium
belle *adj* beautiful
une **belle-mère** *nf* a step-mother
bête *adj* silly
beurk! yuck!
le **beurre** *nm* butter
beurrer *v* to butter
une **bibliothèque** *nf* a library
bien well, good
bientôt soon
bienvenue welcome
un **billet** *nm* **a** ticket
la **biographie** *nf* biography
la **biologie** *nf* biology
un **biscuit** *nm* a biscuit
blanc/blanche *adj* white
un **blanc** *nm* a gap
bleu/bleue *adj* blue
blond/blonde *adj* blond
une **blouse** *nf* an overall
le **bœuf** *nm* beef
bof! so so, dunno!
boire *v* to drink
une **boisson** *nf* a drink
une **boîte** *nf* a box, a tin
un **bol** *nm* a bowl
bon/bonne *adj* good
Bon anniversaire! Happy birthday!
Bon appétit! Enjoy your meal!
un **bonbon** *nm* a sweet
bonjour hello

une **boum** *nf* a party
un **bout** *nm* a bit, an end
une **bouteille** *nf* a bottle
les **boutons** *nm pl* spots
Bravo! Well done!
le **bricolage** *nm* DIY
briller *v* to shine
brosser *v* to brush
le **brouillard** *nm* fog
un **brouillon** *nm* a rough copy
au brouillon in rough
un **bruit** *nm* a noise
brun/brune *adj* dark-haired
une **bûche de Noël** *nf* a Christmas log
une **bulle** *nf* a bubble
un **bureau** *nm* a desk, an office
le **bus** *nm* bus
le **but** *nm* the goal, the aim

c', ce it, that
ça it, that
Ça va? How are you?
Ça va. I'm fine.
cacher *v* to hide
un **cadeau** *nm* a present
un **cadran** *nm* a dial
un **café** *nm* a coffee, a café
un **café-tabac** *nm* a café (which also sells stamps)
une **cafétéria** *nf* a cafeteria
un **cahier** *nm* an exercise book
une **caisse** *nf* a cashdesk, a till
une **caissière** *nf* a cashier
une **calculatrice** *nf* a calculator
calme *adj* calm
un/une **camarade** *nm/nf* a school friend
la **campagne** *nf* the countryside
un **camping** *nm* a campsite
le **Canada** *nm* Canada
canadien/canadienne *adj* Canadian
un **canari** *nm* a canary
la **cantine** *nf* the canteen
le **capitaine** *nm* captain
la **capitale** *nf* the capital
un **car** *nm* a coach
le **caractère** *nm* character
un **carnaval** *nm* a carnival
les **Carambars** *nm pl* French sweets
une **carotte** *nf* a carrot
un **cartable** *nm* a schoolbag
une **carte** *nf* a map, a card
une **carte d'identité** *nf* an identity card
le **carton** *nm* cardboard
une **case** *nf* a square (on a game board), a hut

un **casque** *nm* a helmet
casse-pieds *adj* a nuisance
un **casse-tête** *nm* a brain-teaser
Ça te dit? Do you fancy it?
une **cave** a cellar
un **CD** *nm* a CD
ce, cet, cette this
célèbre *adj* famous
cent hundred
un **centime** *nm* a euro cent (unit of currency)
le **centre** *nm* the centre
un **centre aéré** *nm* **a** children's outdoor activity centre
un centre commercial *nm* an indoor shopping centre
un centre sportif *nm* a sports centre
le **centre-ville** *nm* the town centre
les **céréales** *nf pl* cereal
un **cerf-volant** *nm* a kite
une **cerise** *nf* cherry
certainement certainly
ces these
c'est it's
C'est tout? Is that all?
à **ne pas manquer** not to be missed
ce n'est pas it isn't
cet this
c'était it was
cette this
chacun/chacune each
une **chaîne** *nf* a TV channel
une **chaise** *nf* a chair
une **chambre** *nf* a bedroom
une **chambre d'hôte** *nf* a bed and breakfast
un **champ** *nm* a field
un **championnat** *nm* **a** championship
la **Chandeleur** *nf* Candlemas (festival)
une **chanson** *nf* a song
chanter *v* to sing
une **chanteuse** *nf* a female singer
chaque each
charmant/charmante *adj* charming
chasser *v* to hunt
un **chat** *nm* a cat
un **château** *nm* a castle
chaud/chaude *adj* hot
chauffé/chauffée *adj* heated
un **chemin** *nm* a path, a way
une **chemise** *nf* a shirt
cher/chère *adj* expensive, dear
chercher *v* to look for
chéri darling

un **cheval** *nm* a horse
les **cheveux** *nm pl* hair
chez (Juliette) at (Juliette's)
un **chien** *nm* a dog
un **chiffre** *nm* a number
la **chimie** *nf* chemistry
un/une **chimiste** *nm/nf* a chemist
la **Chine** *nf* China
chinois/chinoise *adj* Chinese
les **chips** *nm pl* crisps
le **chocolat** *nm* chocolate
les **chocos** *nm pl* chocolate biscuits
choisir *v* to choose
une **chose** *nf* a thing
un **chou** *nm* a cabbage
une **chouette** *nf* an owl
chouette! great!
un **chou-fleur** *nm* a cauliflower
une **cicatrice** *nf* a scar
le **ciel** *nm* the sky
le **cinéma** *nm* the cinema
cinq five
cinquante fifty
la **circulation** *nf* traffic
les **ciseaux** *nm pl* scissors
un **citron** *nm* a lemon
une **classe** *nf* a form, a class
un **classeur** *nm* a folder
un **clavier électronique** *nm* an electronic keyboard
une **clé USB** *nf* a memory stick
le **climat** *nm* the climate
le **club des jeunes** *nm* youth club
un **coca** *nm* a cola
cocher *v* to tick
un **cochon d'Inde** *nm* a guinea pig
un **cœur** *nm* a heart
la **coiffure** *nf* hairstyle, hair
un **coin** *nm* a corner
la **colle** *nf* glue
coller *v* to stick
le **collège** *nm* high school
une **colonie de vacances** *nf* a holiday camp (for young people)
combien how much, how many
une **comédie** *nf* a comedy programme/film
un **comédien** *nm* an actor (male)
une **comédienne** *nf* an actress
une **commande** *nf* an order
comme as, like
commencer *v* to start
comment how
une **commode** *nf* a chest of drawers
comparer *v* to compare
compléter *v* to complete
comprendre *v* to understand
compter *v* to count

un **concombre** *nm* a cucumber
un **concours** *nm* a competition
la **confiture** *nf* jam
confortable *adj* comfortable
connaître *v* to know
un **conseil** *nm* a piece of advice
les **conserves** *nf pl* tinned food
une **console** *nf* a games console
une **consonne** *nf* a consonant
content/contente *adj* happy
continuer *v* to continue
le **contraire** *nm* the opposite
contre against
un **copain** *nm* a (boy)friend
une **copine** *nf* a (girl)friend
le **corps** *nm* the body
un/une **correspondant/correspondante** *nm/nf* a penpal
correspondre *v* to correspond with, write to
corriger *v* to correct
à **côté de** beside
se **coucher** *v* to go to bed
la **couleur** *nf* the colour
la **Coupe du Monde** World Cup
un **couplet** *nm* a verse
une **cour** *nf* a courtyard, playground
courageux/courageuse *adj* brave
un **coureur** *nm* a runner
une **couronne** *nf* a crown
le **courrier** *nm* the mail
un **cours** *nm* a lesson
la **course** *nf* the race (track)
les **courses** *nf pl* the shopping
court/courte *adj* short
le **couscous** *nm* couscous
un **cousin** *nm* a cousin (male)
une **cousine** *nf* a cousin (female)
un **coussin** *nm* a cushion
coûter *v* to cost
un **crayon** *nm* a pencil
créer *v* to create
la **crème** *nf* cream
le **créole** *nm* a language formed by a mix of French with local dialects
une **crêpe** *nf* a pancake
une **crêperie** *nf* a pancake restaurant
une **crevette** *nf* a prawn
un **crocodile** *nm* a crocodile
un **croque-monsieur** *nm* a toasted ham and cheese sandwich
les **crottes** *nf pl* droppings
la **cuisine** *nf* the kitchen, cooking
curieux/curieuse *adj* curious

D

d'abord first
d'accord OK
dangereux/dangereuse *adj* dangerous
dans in
la **danse** *nf* dance
danser *v* to dance
la **date** *nf* the date
une **datte** *nf* a date (fruit)
de from, of
un **dé** *nm* a die
débarrasser la table *v* to clear the table
debout standing up
décembre December
déclarer *v* to declare
décorer *v* to decorate
découper *v* to cut out
découvrir *v* to discover
décrire *v* to describe
un **défaut** *nm* a fault
la **défense** *nf* defence
déjà already
le **déjeuner** *nm* lunch
délicieux/délicieuse *adj* delicious
demain tomorrow
demander *v* to ask
un **demi** *nm* half
un **demi-frère** *nm* a half-brother, a step-brother
une **demi-sœur** *nf* a half-sister, a step-sister
un/une **dentiste** *nm/nf* a dentist
les **dents** *nf pl* teeth
le **départ** *nm* the start
un **département français** *nm* a French 'county'
se **déplacer** *v* to move around
un **dépliant** *nm* a leaflet
depuis since
dernier/dernière *adj* last
derrière behind
désiré/désirée *adj* desired
désirer *v* to wish for, desire
désolé/désolée *adj* sorry
le **désordre** *nm* mess
un **dessert** *nm* a dessert
le **dessin** *nm* art
un **dessin** *nm* a drawing
un **dessin animé** *nm* a cartoon
dessiner *v* to draw
détester *v* to hate
deux two
le **deux mars** the second of March
deuxième *adj* second

devant in front of
deviner *v* to guess
les **devoirs** *nm pl* homework
un **dictionnaire** *nm* a dictionary
difficile *adj* difficult
dimanche Sunday
une **dinde** *nf* a turkey
le **dîner** *nm* dinner
dire *v* to say
en **direct** live
discuter *v* to discuss
divorcé/divorcée *adj* divorced
dix ten
le **docteur** *nm* doctor
un **documentaire** *nm* a documentary
le **doigt** *nm* finger
le **domicile** *nm* home
dommage pity
donner *v* to give
dormir *v* to sleep
une **douche** *nf* a shower
se **doucher** *v* to have a shower
douze twelve
le **droit** *nm* the right
le **drapeau** *nm* flag
drôle *adj* funny
dur/dure *adj* hard
dynamique *adj* dynamic

E

l' **eau** *nf* water
l'**eau minérale** *nf* mineral water
un **échange** *nm* an exchange
échanger *v* to swap
échauffer *v* to warm up
les **échecs** *nm pl* chess
une **école** *nf* a school
l'**école maternelle** *nf* nursery school
l'**école primaire** *nf* primary school
écolo *adj* environmentally-friendly
écossais/écossaise *adj* Scottish
l' **Écosse** *nf* Scotland
écouter *v* to listen
un **écran** *nm* a screen
écrire *v* to write
l' **écriture** *nf* (hand)writing
efficace *adj* efficient
une **église** *nf* a church
égoïste *adj* selfish
électrique *adj* electric
un **éléphant** *nm* an elephant
un/une **élève** *nm/nf* a pupil
elle she, it
un **email** *nm* an email
Je t' **embrasse** With love (to end a letter)

une **émission** *nf* a programme
une **émission de télé réalité** *nf*
 a reality TV programme
une **émission musicale** *nf*
 a music programme
une **émission sportive** *nf*
 a sports programme
l' **empereur** *nm* emperor
un **emploi** *nm* a job
un **emploi du temps** *nm* a timetable
emprunter *v* to borrow
en in
encore again, more
un **endroit** *nm* a place
un **enfant** *nm* a child
enfin at last
l' **ennui** *nm* boredom
ennuyeux/ennuyeuse *adj* boring
énorme *adj* enormous
une **enquête** *nf* a survey
enregistrer *v* to record
ensemble together
ensuite then
entendre *v* to hear
entêté/entêtée *adj* stubborn
l' **entraînement** *nm* training
un/une **entraîneur/entraîneuse** *nm/f*
 a coach (sport)
entre between
une **entrée** *nf* a starter, a hallway
j'ai **envie de** I feel like
environ about, approximately
épeler *v* to spell
un **épicier** *nm* a grocer
les **épinards** *nm pl* spinach
l' **EPS = l' éducation physique et sportive** *nf* PE/games
une **équipe** *nf* a team
bien équipé well equipped
l' **équitation** *nf* horse riding
une **erreur** *nf* a mistake
tu **es** you are
l' **escalade** *nf* mountain climbing
un **escargot** *nm* a snail
l' **espace** *nf or nm* space
l' **Espagne** *nf* Spain
espagnol/espagnole *adj* Spanish
l' **espagnol** *nm* Spanish
espérer *v* to hope, to wish
l' **essence** *nf* petrol
il/elle/on **est** he/she/it is, we are
l' **est** *nm* the east
et and
Et toi? How about you?
un **étage** *nm* a storey, a floor
une **étagère** *nf* a shelf
il **était** he/it was
les **États-Unis** *nm pl* the United States

l' **été** *nm* summer
vous **êtes** you are
une **étoile** *nf* a star
étranger, étrangère *adj* foreign
être *v* to be
les **études** *nf pl* studies
un **étudiant** *nm* a student (male)
une **étudiante** *nf* a student (female)
euh erm (used for hesitation)
un **euro** *nm* a euro (unit of currency)
l' **Europe** *nf* Europe
éviter *v* to miss/avoid
excusez-moi excuse me
un **exemple** *nm* an example
exister *v* to exist
une **explication** *nf* an explanation
expliquer *v* to explain
une **exposition** *nf* an exhibition
une **expression-clé** *nf* a key expression
un **extrait** *nm* an extract
extraordinaire *adj* extraordinary

Ⓕ

fabriquer *v* to make
en **face de** opposite
facile *adj* easy
la **faim** *nf* hunger
j'ai faim I'm hungry
faire *v* to make, to do
faire la cuisine *v* to do the cooking
faire la vaisselle *v* to do the washing up
faire le ménage *v* to do the housework
faire mon lit *v* to make my bed
je/tu **fais** I/you make, do
nous **faisons** we make, do
il/elle/on **fait** he/she/it makes/does, we make/do
en **fait** in fact
vous **faites** you make, do
familial/familiale *adj* family
une **famille** *nf* a family
un/une **fan** *nm/nf* a fan
un **fantôme** *nm* a ghost
la **farine** *nf* flour
le **fast-food** *nm* fast food restaurant
fatigant/fatigante *adj* tiring
il **faut** you have to, you ought to
faux/fausse *adj* false, wrong
favori/favorite *adj* favourite
félicitations! congratulations!
féminin/féminine *adj* feminine
une **fenêtre** *nf* a window
une **ferme** *nf* a farm
fermé/fermée *adj* shut, closed
fermer *v* to close

une **fête** *nf* a party, a festival
fêter *v* to celebrate
une **feuille** *nf* a sheet of paper, a leaf
un **feuilleton** *nm* a soap opera
un **feutre** *nm* a felt-tip pen
les **feux** *nm pl* traffic lights
une **fève** *nf* a bean, a charm
février February
une **fiche** *nf* a form
fidèle *adj* faithful
un **filet** *nm* a net
une **fille** *nf* a girl, a daughter
fille unique *nf* an only child (girl)
un **film** *nm* a film
les **films de guerre** *nm pl* war films
les films d'action *nm pl* action films
les films de science-fiction *nm pl* science fiction films
un **fils** *nm* a son
fils unique *nm* an only child (boy)
la **fin** *nf* the end
finalement finally
fini/finie *adj* finished
finir *v* to finish
une **fleur** *nf* a flower
un/une **fleuriste** *nm/nf* a florist
la **FNAC** *nf* name of a chain of shops that sells DVDs, CDs, books, etc.
à **fond** really loud
mettre ma musique à fond to turn my music up loud
ils/elles **font** they make, do
le **foot(ball)** *nm* football
le **footballeur** *nm* footballer
en **forme** *adj* healthy
formidable *adj* great, fantastic
fort/forte *adj* strong
fou/folle *adj* mad
un **four** *nm* an oven
un **foyer** *nm* a home
frais/fraîche *adj* fresh
une **fraise** *nf* a strawberry
le **français** *nm* French
français/française *adj* French
francophone *adj* French-speaking
un **frère** *nm* a brother
un **frigo** *nm* a fridge
frisé/frisée *adj* curly
des **frites** *nf pl* chips
froid/froide *adj* cold
le **fromage** *nm* cheese
le **front** *nm* forehead
un **fruit** *nm* a fruit
les **fruits de mer** *nm pl* seafood

gagner *v* to win, to earn
une **galerie** *nf* a gallery
une **galette** *nf* a cake, a pancake
la galette des Rois *nf* special cake
eaten on 6 January
gallois/galloise adj Welsh
un **garçon** *nm* a boy
garder des enfants *v* to look after
children
une **gare SNCF** *nf* a railway station
un **gâteau** *nm* a cake
gazeux/gazeuse *adj* fizzy
une boisson gazeuse a fizzy drink
geler *v* to freeze
en **général** in general
le **général** *nm* general
généralement generally
généreux/généreuse *adj*
generous
génial/géniale *adj* great, fantastic
des **gens** *nm pl* people
gentil/gentille *adj* nice, kind
la **géographie** *nf* geography
un **geste** *nm* a gesture, a movement
un **gîte** *nm* holiday cottage
une **glace** *nf* an ice cream
un **glossaire** *nm* a glossary
une **gomme** *nf* a rubber
un **goûter** *nm* an afternoon snack
un **gouvernement** *nm* a government
la **grammaire** *nf* grammar
un **gramme** *nm* a gram
grand/grande *adj* big, tall
la **Grande-Bretagne** *nf* Great Britain
une **grand-mère** *nf* a grandmother
un **grand-père** *nm* a grandfather
les **grands-parents** *nm pl*
grandparents
gras/grasse *adj* fatty, greasy
en gras in bold
gratuit/gratuite *adj* free
une **grille** *nf* a grid
grillé/grillée *adj* grilled, toasted
gris/grise *adj* grey
gros/grosse *adj* plump, fat
une **guitare** *nf* a guitar
la **gym** *nf* gymnastics, exercises
le **gymnase** *nm* gymnasium

s' **habiller** *v* to get dressed
un **habitant** *nm* an inhabitant
habiter *v* to live
un **hamburger** *nm* a hamburger
un **hamster** *nm* a hamster

le **hand-ball** *nm* handball
haut/haute *adj* high, tall
à haute voix aloud
un **héros** *nm* a hero
hésiter *v* to hesitate
une **heure** *nf* an hour
à deux heures at two o'clock
heureux/heureuse *adj* happy
un **hibou** *nm* an owl
hier yesterday
le **hindi** *nm* Hindi
l' **histoire** *nf* history
l' **hiver** *nm* winter
la **honte** *nf* shame
un **hôpital** *nm* a hospital
j'ai **horreur de...** I hate...
horrible *adj* terrible, awful
un **hot-dog** *nm* a hot dog
un **hôtel** *nm* a hotel
l' **huile d'olive** *nf* olive oil
huit eight
une **huître** *nf* an oyster
une **humeur** *nf* a mood, humour
hystérique *adj* hysterical

ici here
idéal/idéale *adj* ideal
une **idée** *nf* an idea
identifier *v* to identify
une **identité** *nf* an identity
il he, it
une **île** *nf* an island
illustré/illustrée *adj* illustrated
il n'y a pas de/d' there isn't/there
aren't
ils they
il y a there is/there are
il y a en a trop there are too
many
une **image** *nf* a picture
imaginer *v* to imagine
un **imbécile** *nm* an imbecile, a fool
imiter *v* to imitate, copy
un **immeuble** *nm* a block of flats
incroyable *adj* unbelievable
indiquer *v* to show
un **infinitif** *nm* an infinitive
les **informations** *nf pl* information, the
news
l' **informatique** *nf* computing, ICT
les **infos** *nf pl* the news
intelligent/intelligente *adj*
intelligent
intéressant/intéressante *adj*
interesting

l' **Internet** *nm* the Internet
interrogatif/interrogative *adj*
interrogative, question
interviewer *v* to interview
l' **intrus** *nm* the odd-one-out
une **invitation** *nf* an invitation
un/une **invité/invitée** *nm/nf* a guest, a
visitor
inviter *v* to invite
l' **Irlande** *nf* Ireland
irlandais/irlandaise *adj* Irish
irrégulier/irrégulière *adj* irregular
l' **Italie** *nf* Italy
italien/italienne *adj* Italian
l' **italien** *nm* Italian

j' I
j'ai I have
j'ai très hâte I can't wait
jamais never
la **jambe** *nf* leg
le **jambon** *nm* ham
janvier January
le **japonais** *nm* Japanese
un **jardin** *nm* a garden
le **jardinage** *nm* gardening
jaune *adj* yellow
je I
un **jean** *nm* a pair of jeans
une **jetée** *nf* a pier, a jetty
jeter *v* to throw
un **jeton** *nm* a counter
un **jeu** *nm* a game
le jeu du morpion *nm* noughts
and crosses
le jeu de sept familles *nm* happy
families
un jeu de société *nm* a board
game
un **jeu télévisé** *nm* a TV gameshow
jeudi Thursday
jeune *adj* young
un/une **jeune** *nm/nf* a young person
les **jeux vidéo** *nm pl* video games
joli/jolie *adj* pretty
jouer *v* to play
un **jouet** *nm* a toy
le/la **joueur/joueuse** *nm/f* player
un **jour** *nm* a day
tous les jours every day
le **jour des Rois** *nm* Epiphany
une **journée** *nf* a day
le **judo** *nm* judo
juillet July
juin June
un **jumeau** *nm* a twin (boy)

un **jus** *nm* a juice
    un **jus d'orange** *nm* an orange juice
    jusqu'à until
    juste fair, just

le **kayak** *nm* kayaking, canoeing
un **kilo** *nm* a kilo
un **kilomètre** *nm* a kilometre
un **kiwi** *nm* a kiwi fruit

    l' the
    la the
    là there
    là-bas over there
un **lac** *nm* a lake
le **lait** *nm* milk
une **lampe** *nf* a lamp
    lancer *v* to throw
une **langue** *nf* a language
un **lapin** *nm* a rabbit
    laquelle n*f* which
(se) **laver** *v* to wash (yourself)
    le the
la **leçon** *nf* lesson
un **lecteur** *nm* a reader (male)
un **lecteur DVD** *nm* a DVD player
une **lectrice** *nf* a reader (female)
la **lecture** *nf* reading
la **légende** *nf* the key (to a map)
les **légumes** *nm pl* vegetables
les **lentilles** *nf pl* lentils
    lequel *m* which
    les the
une **lettre** *nf* a letter
    leur their
    lever *v* to lift, raise
se **lever** *v* to get up
une **limonade** *nf* a lemonade
    lire *v* to read
une **liste** *nf* a list
une **liste d'achats** *nf* a shopping list
un **lit** *nm* a bed
un **litre** *nm* a litre
un **livre** *nm* a book
    loger *v* to stay
    loin far
les **loisirs** *nm pl* leisure
    Londres London
    long/longue *adj* long
    lourd/lourde *adj* heavy
    lui him
    lundi Monday
la **lune** *nf* the moon

des **lunettes** *nf pl* glasses
le **lycée** *nm* sixth form college

    ma my
une **machine à karaoké** *nf* a karaoke machine
les **mâchoires** *nf pl* jaws
    madame Mrs, madam
    mademoiselle Miss
un **magasin** *nm* a shop
un **magazine** *nm* a magazine
la **magie** *nf* magic
    mai May
    mais but
une **maison** *nf* a house
    à la maison at home
une **majorité** *nf* a majority
    mal badly
    ça va mal things aren't going very well, I don't feel well
j'ai **mal (aux dents)** I've got (tooth) ache
    malade ill
la **malédiction** *nf* curse
    maman *nf* mum, mummy
    mamie *nf* granny
la **Manche** the English Channel
    manger *v* to eat
un **mannequin** *nm* a model
    manquer *v* to miss
le **maquillage** *nm* make up
un **marché** *nm* a market
    mardi Tuesday
le **Mardi Gras** *nm* Shrove Tuesday
    marin *adj* of the sea
    marquer un but/un panier to score a goal/a basket
    marrant/marrante *adj* funny
    marron *adj* brown
    mars March
    masculin/masculine *adj* masculine
un **masque** *nm* a mask
un **match** *nm* a match
un **match de foot** *nm* a football match
les **mathématiques/maths** *nf pl* maths
une **matière** *nf* a subject
le **matin** *nm* morning
    mauvais/mauvaise *adj* bad
    il fait mauvais the weather's dull
la **mayonnaise** *nf* mayonnaise
    méchant/méchante *adj* naughty, evil
    méfiant/méfiante *adj* suspicious
    meilleur/meilleure *adj* best
    mélanger *v* to mix

la **mêlée** *nf* scrum (rugby)
un **membre** *nm* a member
    même same, even
la **mémoire** *nf* memory
    mémoriser *v* to memorise, learn by heart
    menacé *adj* threatened
    mentionné/mentionnée *adj* mentioned
la **mer** *nf* the sea
    merci thank you
    mercredi Wednesday
une **mère** *nf* a mother
    mes my
la **messe** *nf* Mass
la **météo** *nf* weather forecast
un **métier** *nm* a job
    mettre *v* to put
    mettre le couvert *v* to set the table
un **meuble** *nm* an item of furniture
    miam! miam! yum!
le **midi** midday, lunchtime
le **miel** *nm* honey
    mieux *adv* better
un **milk-shake** *nm* a milkshake
un **mime** *nm* a mime
    mince *adj* thin, slim
le **mini-golf** *nm* miniature golf
    mignon/mignonne *adj* cute
le **ministère** *nm* ministry
    minuit midnight
un **miroir** *nm* a mirror
la **mobylette** *nf* moped
un **modèle** *nm* a model
    moderne *adj* modern
    moi me
    moi aussi me too
    moi non plus me neither
    moins less
    au moins at least
    moins que less than
un **mois** *nm* a month
en ce **moment** at the moment
    mon my
le **monde** *nm* the world
    tout le monde everybody
un/une **moniteur/monitrice** *nm/f* a youth leader
    monsieur Mr, sir
à la **montagne** in the mountains
    monter *v* **la tente** to put up the tent
une **montre** *nf* a watch
    montrer *v* to show
la **moquette** *nf* carpet
un **morceau** *nm* a piece
    mort/morte *adj* dead
un **mot** *nm* a word

un **mot apparenté** *nm* a cognate
un **mot-clé** *nm* a key word
les **moules marinière** *nf pl*
    mussels cooked in white wine
un **mouton** *nm* a sheep
le **moyen** *nm* **the** means
  moyen/moyenne *adj* average
un **mur** *nm* a wall
la **musculation** *nf* body-building
un **musée** *nm* a museum
la **musique** *nf* music

la **naissance** *nf* birth
la **natation** *nf* swimming
la **nationalité** *nf* nationality
la **nature** *nf* nature
  né/née *adj* born
  négatif/négative *adj* negative
la **neige** *nf* snow
il **neige** it's snowing
  neuf nine
un **nez** *nm* a nose
le **Noël** *nm* Christmas
  noir/noire *adj* black
un **nom** *nm* a name, noun
un **nombre** *nm* a number
  nombreux/nombreuse *adj*
    numerous, many
  nommer *v* to name
  non no
le **nord** *nm* the north
  le nord-est *nm* the north-east
  le nord-ouest *nm* the north-west
  normalement normally
  nos our
  noter *v* to note
  nous we, us
  nouveau/nouvelle *adj* new
une **nouveauté** *nf* a novelty/new thing
  novembre November
  nul nil
  c'est nul it's rubbish
des **nuages** *nm pl* clouds
un **numéro** *nm* a number, an edition
    (of a magazine)
  numéroter *v* to number

un **objet** *nm* an object
  observer *v* to observe
  occupée *adj* busy
s' **occuper de** *v* to look after
  octobre October
un **œil** *nm* an eye
un **œuf** *nm* an egg

un **office du tourisme** *nm* a tourist
    office
  officiel/officielle *adj* official
une **offre** *nf* an offer
  offrir *v* to offer, give as a present
un **oiseau** *nm* a bird
une **omelette** *nf* an omelette
  on we, they, one
un **oncle** *nm* an uncle
ils/elles **ont** they have
  onze eleven
une **opinion** *nf* an opinion
  optimiste *adj* optimistic
un **orage** *nm* a storm
une **orange** *nf* an orange
un **ordinateur** *nm* a computer
un **ordre** *nm* an order
  dans le bon ordre in the right
    order
les **ordures** *nf pl* rubbish
  organiser *v* to organise
un **orphelin** *nm* an orphan
l' **orthographe** *nf* spelling
  ou or
  où where
  Ouah! Wow!
l' **ouest** *nm* the west
  oui yes
un **ouragan** *nm* a hurricane
  ouvert/ouverte *adj* open
  ouvrir *v* to open

la **page** *nf* page
le **pain** *nm* bread
une **paire** *nf* a pair
un **pamplemousse** *nm* a grapefruit
un **panier** *nm* a basket
la **panique** *nf* panic
  paniquer *v* to panic
le **papier** *nm* paper
  Pâques *nm pl* Easter
un **paquet** *nm* a packet
  par by
un **paragraphe** *nm* a paragraph
un **parc** *nm* a park
  parce que because
  pardon sorry
les **parents** *nm pl* parents
  paresseux/paresseuse *adj* lazy
  parfois sometimes
un **parfum** *nm* a perfume, flavour
le **parking** *nm* car park
le **parlement** *nm* parliament
  parler *v* to talk
  parmi among
une **part** *nf* a portion, slice

  partager *v* to share
un/une **partenaire** *nm/nf* a partner
  participer *v* to take part
  partir *v* to leave
  partout everywhere
  pas not
  pas moi not me
  passer *v* to spend time
  passer l'aspirateur *v* to do the
    vacuuming
un **passe-temps** *nm* a hobby
une **passion** *nf* a hobby
le **pâté** *nm* pâté
  patient/patiente *adj* patient
le **patin à roulettes** *nm* roller-
    skating
le **patinage** *nm* ice-skating
une **patinoire** *nf* an ice rink
  pauvre *adj* poor
un **pays** *nm* a country
le **pays de Galles** *nm* Wales
la **pêche** *nf* fishing
une **peinture** *nf* a painting
  pendant during
une **pendule** *nf* a clock
  pénible *adj* awful
  penser *v* to think
  perdre *v* to lose
  perdre de vue to lose sight of
  perdu/perdue *adj* lost
un **père** *nm* a father
un **perroquet** *nm* a parrot
une **perruche** *nf* a budgerigar
un **personnage** *nm* a character
la **personnalité** *nf* personality
une **personne-mystère** *nf* a mystery
    person
la **pétanque** *nf* type of bowls game
  petit/petite *adj* small
une **petite amie** *nf* girlfriend
le **petit déjeuner** *nm* breakfast
des **petits pois** *nm pl* peas
un **peu** a little
il/elle/on **peut** he/she/it/we can
ils/elles **peuvent** they can
je/tu **peux** I/you can
une **pharmacie** *nf* a chemist's
une **photo** *nf* a photograph
une **phrase** *nf* a sentence
la **physique** *nf* physics
  physiquement physically
une **pièce** *nf* a room, a coin
un **pied** *nm* a foot
le **ping-pong** *nm* table tennis
un **pique-nique** *nm* a picnic
  pire *adv* worse
le/la **pire** the worst
une **piscine** *nf* a swimming pool

la **pizza** *nf* pizza
une **pizzeria** *nf* a pizzeria
une **plage** *nf* a beach
plaît: s'il te/vous plaît please
un **plan** *nm* a map
la **planche à voile** *nf* windsurfing
le **plancher** *nm* floor
le **plat** *nm* a dish, a plate
plein/pleine *adj* full
en plein air outdoors
il **pleut** it's raining
plier *v* to bend
la **plongée** *nf* diving
pluriel/plurielle *adj* plural
plus more
plusieurs several
plus que more than
un **poème** *nm* a poem
le **poil** *nm* hair (on an animal)
un **poisson** *nm* a fish
le **poivre** *nm* pepper
poli/polie *adj* polite
la **police** *nf* the police
un **policier** *nm* a detective film, a police officer
poliment politely
une **pomme** *nf* an apple
le **porc** *nm* pork
un **port** *nm* a harbour, a port
un **portable** *nm* a mobile phone
une **porte** *nf* a door
porter *v* to wear
poser *v* to put
positif/positive *adj* positive
la **poste** *nf* the post office
un **poster** *nm* a poster
une **poule** *nf* a chicken
le **poulet** *nm* chicken meat
une **poupée** *nf* a doll
pour for
pourquoi why
la **poursuite** *nf* pursuit
pratique *adj* practical
préféré/préférée *adj* favourite
la **préférence** *nf* preference
préférer *v* to prefer
un **préfet** *nm* a prefect
premier/première *adj* first
prendre *v* to take
les **préparatifs** *nm pl* preparations
préparer *v* to prepare
près de near
un/une **présentateur/présentatrice** *nm/f* a TV presenter
présenter *v* to present
presque nearly
le **printemps** *nm* spring
un **prix** *nm* a price, a prize

un **problème** *nm* a problem
prochain/prochaine *adj* next
proche close, near
un/une **prof** *nm/nf* a teacher
un **professeur** *nm* a teacher
un **projet** *nm* a project
une **promenade** *nf* a walk
prononcer *v* to pronounce
la **prononciation** *nf* pronunciation
propre *adj* clean
la **prudence** *nf* prudence, cautiousness
publicitaire advertising
une **publicité** *nf* an advertisement
puis then
la **purée** *nf* mashed potato

le **quai** *nm* platform
la **qualité** *nf* quality
quand when
une **quantité** *nf* a quantity
quarante forty
un **quart** *nm* a quarter
un **quartier** *nm* an area
quatorze fourteen
quatre four
quatre-vingts eighty
quatre-vingt-deux eighty-two
quatre-vingt-dix ninety
que that, what, which
québécois/québécoise *adj* from Quebec
quel/quelle which
quelque chose something
quelquefois sometimes
quelques some, a few
quelqu'un somebody
qu'est-ce que what
une **question** *nf* a question
qui who
quinze fifteen
quitter *v* to leave
quoi what
quotidien/quotidienne *adj* daily

R

le **racisme** *nm* racism
raconter *v* to tell
la **radio** *nf* radio
le **rafting** *nm* white-water rafting
raide *adj* straight
raisonnable *adj* reasonable
la **randonnée** *nf* hiking
ranger *v* to tidy, put away
râpé/râpée *adj* grated

un **rappel** *nm* a reminder
rapper *v* to rap
rassurer *v* to reassure
un **rat** *nm* a rat
la **réception** *nf* reception
se **réchauffer** *v* to warm up
rechercher *v* to look for
recopier *v* to copy out
un **record** *nm* a record
la **récréation** *nf* breaktime
reculer *v* to move back
la **rédaction** *nf* the editorial team
une **rédaction** *nf* an essay
réécouter *v* to listen again
un **refrain** *nm* a chorus
regarder *v* to look, watch
un **régime** *nm* a diet
une **région** *nf* an area, a region
une **règle** *nf* a ruler, a rule
régulier/régulière *adj* regular
une **reine** *nf* a queen
relaxer *v* to relax
relier *v* to join
la **religion** *nf* religion, RE
relis reread
remets put back
remplir *v* to fill in
un **renard** *nm* a fox
une **rencontre** *nf* a meeting, an encounter
un **rendez-vous** *nm* a meeting, a date
les **renseignements** *nm pl* information
la **rentrée** *nf* first day back at school (September)
rentrer *v* to return
un **repas** *nm* a meal
répéter *v* to repeat
répondre *v* to answer, to reply
une **réponse** *nf* an answer
un **reportage** *nm* a report
reposant/reposante *adj* restful
respirer *v* to breathe
ressembler à *v* to look like
un **restaurant** *nm* a restaurant
rester *v* to stay
un **résultat** *nm* a result
en **retard** late
retrouver *v* to meet
une **réunion** *nf* a meeting
un **rêve** *nm* a dream
se **réveiller** *v* to wake up
rêveur/rêveuse *adj* dreamy
réviser *v* to revise
au **revoir** goodbye
revoir *v* to see again
le **rez-de-chaussée** *nm* ground floor
des **rideaux** *nm pl* curtains

(ne...) rien nothing
rigolo *adj* funny
le riz *nm* rice
un roi *nm* a king
rond/ronde *adj* round
rose *adj* pink
un rôti *nm* a roast
rouge *adj* red
rougir *v* to blush
une route *nf* a road, route
roux/rousse *adj* red-haired
une rue *nf* a street
le rugby *nm* rugby

S

sa his, her
un sac *nm* a bag
un sac à dos *nm* a rucksack
la Saint-Valentin *nf* Valentine's Day
je/tu sais I/you know
une saison *nf* a season
il/elle/on sait he/she it knows, we know
une salade *nf* a salad, a lettuce
une salle *nf* a room
une salle à manger *nf* a dining room
une salle de bains *nf* a bathroom
un salon *nm* a living room
saluer *v* to greet
salut hello
samedi Saturday
un sandwich *nm* a sandwich
un sandwich au fromage *nm* a cheese sandwich
un sandwich au jambon *nm* a ham sandwich
sans without
s'appeler *v* to be called
sauf except
le saumon *nm* salmon
sauter *v* to jump
les sciences *nf pl* science
scolaire *adj* school
une séance *nf* a performance, a meeting
secouer *v* to shake
le secours *nm* help, aid
Au secours! Help!
sec/sèche *adj* dry
seize sixteen
un séjour *nm* a living room, a stay
le sel *nm* salt
une semaine *nf* a week
le Sénégal *nm* Senegal
sénégalais/sénégalaise *adj* Senegalese
sept seven
septembre September

une série *nf* a series
sérieux/sérieuse *adj* serious
un serpent *nm* a snake
ses his, her
seulement only
si if
un siècle *nm* a century
un signe particulier *nm* a feature
silencieux/silencieuse *adj* silent
simple *adj* simple
singulier/singulière *adj* singular
un site web *nm* a website
six six
sixième *adj* sixth
le skate *nm* skateboarding, skateboard
le ski *nm* skiing
snob posh
une sœur *nf* a sister
la soif *nf* thirst
j'ai soif I'm thirsty
un soir *nm* an evening
une soirée *nf* an evening
soixante sixty
soixante-dix seventy
le soleil *nm* the sun
sombre *adj* dark
nous sommes we are
son his, her
un sondage *nm* a survey
ils/elles sont they are
une sortie *nf* an outing, an exit
sortir *v* to go out
souligné/soulignée *adj* underlined
une soupe *nf* a soup
une souris *nf* a mouse
sous under
le sous-sol *nm* basement
souvent often
les spaghetti *nm pl* spaghetti
spécial/spéciale *adj* special
la spécialité *nf* speciality
un spectacle *nm* a show
un/une spectateur/spectatrice *nm/f* a spectator
le sport *nm* sport
sportif/sportive *adj* sporty
un stade *nm* a stadium
un/une stagiaire *nm/f* a trainee
une star *nf* a star, a celebrity
un steak-frites *nm* steak and chips
studieux/studieuse *adj* studious
un stylo *nm* a pen
le sucre *nm* sugar
le sucre en poudre *nm* caster sugar
sucré/sucrée *adj* sweet
le sud *nm* the south
le sud-est *nm* the south-east

le sud-ouest *nm* the south-west
je suis I am
la Suisse *nf* Switzerland
suisse *adj* Swiss
suivant/suivante *adj* following
à suivre to be continued
un sujet *nm* a subject
super great
un supermarché *nm* a supermarket
sur on
sûr/sûre *adj* sure, certain
surfer *v* to surf
surtout especially
un/une surveillant/surveillante *nm/f* an invigilator, a superviser (in a school)
sympa *adj* kind, nice
un symptôme *nm* a symptom

T

ta your
une table *nf* a table
un tableau *nm* a board, a picture
une table de chevet *nf* a bedside table
un tableau blanc *nm* a whiteboard
une tâche *nf* a task
une tache de rousseur *nf* a freckle
la taille *nf* size
un taille-crayon *nm* a pencil sharpener
un tambour *nm* a drum
une tante *nf* an aunt
un tapis *nm* a rug
tard *adv* late
une tarte *nf* a tart, a pie
une tartine *nf* a slice of bread and butter
une tasse *nf* a cup
tâter *v* to feel
le taxi *nm* taxi
la technologie *nf* technology, D&T
télécharger *v* to download
la télé numérique *nf* digital TV
le téléphone *nm* the telephone
la télé(vision) *nf* TV, television
à la télévision on television
le temps *nm* the weather, time
le temps libre *nm* free time
le tennis *nm* tennis
les tennis *nm pl* trainers
tendre *adj* tender
terminer *v* to finish, to end
le terrain *nm* pitch
par terre on the ground
la terreur *nf* terror
terrifiant/terrifiante *adj* terrifying
tes your

le **test de mémoire** *nm* memory
  test
têtu/têtue *adj* stubborn
un **texte** *nm* a text
le **TGV** *nm* French high-speed train
un **thé** *nm* a cup of tea
un **théâtre** *nm* a theatre
le **thon** *nm* tuna
un **ticket de loterie** *nm* a lottery
  ticket
timide *adj* shy
un **titre** *nm* a title
toi you
les **toilettes** *nf pl* the toilets
une **tomate** *nf* a tomato
tomber *v* to fall
ton your
toucher *v* to touch
toujours always
un **tour** *nm* a trip
une **tour** *nf* a tower
à **tour de rôle** in turn
un **touriste** *nm* a tourist
touristique *adj* for tourists
tourner *v* to turn
tous all
tout/toute all
une **traduction** *nf* a translation
le **train** *nm* train
une **tranche** *nf* a slice
le **travail** *nm* work
travailler *v* to work
travailleur/travailleuse *adj* hard-
  working
traverser *v* to cross
treize thirteen
trembler *v* to tremble
trente thirty
très very
triste *adj* sad
trois three
le **trois mai** the third of May
troisième *adj* third
trop too
une **trousse** *nf* a pencil-case
trouver *v* to find
le **truc** *nm* thing
la **truite** *nf* trout
tu you (to a friend or close
  relative)
typique *adj* typical

un/une **a, an, one**
une **unité** *nf* a unit
l' **univers** *nm* the universe
une **usine** *nf* a factory
utiliser *v* to use

il/elle/on **va** he/she/it goes, we go
les **vacances** *nf pl* holidays
je **vais** I go
la **vanille** *nf* vanilla
tu **vas** you go
une **vedette** *nf* a star
un **vélo** *nm* a bike
le **vélo** *nm* cycling
vendredi Friday
venir *v* to come
le **vent** *nm* wind
la **vente** *nf* sale
un **verbe** *nm* a verb
vérifier *v* to check
un **verre** *nm* a glass
vert/verte *adj* green
les **vêtements** *nm pl* clothes
il/elle/on **veut** he/she/it wants, we want
je **veux** I want
la **viande** *nf* meat
une **vidéo** *nf* a video
Je **viens de...** I come from...
vieux/vieille *adj* old
un **village** *nm* a village
une **ville** *nf* a town
en ville in town, into town
le **vin** *nm* wine
vingt twenty
violent/violente *adj* violent
une **visite** *nf* a visit
visiter *v* to visit
vite quick
vivre *v* to live
le **vocabulaire** *nm* vocabulary
voici here is, are
voilà there is, are
la **voile** *nf* sailing
voir *v* to see
un/une **voisin/voisine** *nm/nf* a neighbour
une **voiture** *nf* a car
une **voix** *nf* a voice
à haute voix aloud
vomir *v* to be sick
ils/elles **vont** they go
vos your
votre your
je/tu **voudrais** I/you would like
il/elle/on **voudrait** he/she/it we would like
vous you (to an adult you don't
  know well, or to more than one
  person)
un **voyage** *nm* a journey
une **voyelle** *nf* a vowel
vrai/vraie *adj* true
vraiment really

le **week-end** *nm* the weekend
un **western** *nm* a western

Y

un **yaourt** *nm* a yoghurt
les **yeux** *nm pl* eyes

A

a un/une
advert une pub(licité) *nf*
a little bit un peu
afternoon l'après-midi *nm*
afternoon tea le goûter *nm*
Algeria l'Algérie *nf*
Algerian algérien/algérienne *adj*
also aussi
always toujours
I **am** je suis
I **am (11).** J'ai (11) ans.
and et
animal(s) un animal (les animaux) *nm*
apple une pomme *nf*
April avril
Are there...? Il y a...?
you **are** tu es *(to a friend or relative)*, vous êtes *(to more than one person, someone you don't know)*
art le dessin *nm*
at à
at the weekends le week-end
athletics l'athlétisme *nm*
August août
aunt la tante *nf*
autumn l'automne *nm*

B

bag le sac *nm*
balcony le balcon *nm*
basement le sous-sol *nm*
bathroom la salle de bains *nf*
to **be** être *v*
beach la plage *nf*
because parce que
bed le lit *nm*
bedroom la chambre *nf*
bedside table une table de chevet *nf*
behind derrière
the **best** la meilleure *f*
the **best** le meilleure *m*
better mieux *adj*
between... (and...) entre... (et...)
big grand/grande *adj*
biology la biologie *nf*
birthday l'anniversaire *nm*
biscuit un biscuit *nm*
a little **bit** un peu
black noir/noire *adj*
block of flats un immeuble *nm*
blond blond/blonde *adj*
blue bleu/bleue *adj*

book le livre *nm*
bookshelf l'étagère *nf*
boring pas marrant, ennuyeux/ ennuyeuse *adj*
bottle une bouteille *nf*
brave courageux/courageuse *adj*
breaktime la récréation *nf*
brother un frère *nm*
brown brun/brune *(hair) adj*, marron *(eyes) adj*
budgie une perruche *nf*
bus le bus *nm*
busy occupé *adj*
but mais
butter le beurre *nm*

C

café le café *nm*
cafeteria une cafétéria *nf*
cake le gâteau *nm*
calculator la calculatrice *nf*
I am **called** je m'appelle
you are **called** tu t'appelles
Canada le Canada *nm*
carpet la moquette *nf*
carrots les carottes *nf pl*
cartoon un dessin animé *nm*
cat un chat *nm*
cellar la cave *nf*
centre le centre *nm*
chair la chaise *nf*
cheese le fromage *nm*
chemist's une pharmacie *nf*
chemistry la chimie *nf*
cherry une cerise *nf*
chest of drawers la commode *nf*
chicken le poulet *nm*
church l'église *nf*
cinema le cinéma *nm*
It is **cloudy.** Il fait gris./Il y a des nuages.
to **clear the table** débarrasser *v* la table
climbing l'escalade *nf*
coach (sport) l'entraîneur/ entraîneuse *nm/f*
coffee le café *nm*
coke le coca *nm*
It is **cold.** Il fait froid.
colour la couleur *nf*
comedy programme/film une comédie *nf*
computer l'ordinateur *nm*
country le pays *nm*
cousin (boy) le cousin *nm*
cousin (girl) la cousine *nf*
crisps les chips *nm pl*
cucumber le concombre *nm*

curly frisé/frisée *adj*
curtains les rideaux *nm pl*
cushion le coussin *nm*
cute mignon/mignonne *adj*
cycling le vélo *nm*
to go **cycling** faire *v* du vélo

D

dancing la danse *nf*
December décembre
desk le bureau *nm*
detective film un film policier *nm*
dictionary le dictionnaire *nm*
difficult difficile *adj*
digital camera un appareil photo numérique *nm*
dining room la salle à manger *nf*
dinner le dîner *nm*
diving la plongée *nf*
to **do** faire *v*
to **do the cooking** faire *v* la cuisine
to **do the housework** faire *v* le ménage
to **do the vacuuming** passer *v* l'aspirateur
to **do the washing up** faire *v* la vaisselle
Do you have ...? Tu as ...? *(to a friend or relative)*, Vous avez...? *(to more than one person, someone you don't know well)*
documentary un documentaire *nm*
dog le chien *nm*
drama l'art dramatique *nm*
to **drink** boire *v*

E

east l'est *nm*
to **eat** manger *v*
eggs les œufs *nm pl*
eight huit
eighteen dix-huit
eighty quatre-vingts
electronic keyboard un clavier électronique *nm*
eleven onze
England l'Angleterre *nf*
essay une rédaction *nf*
English anglais/anglaise *adj*
(in the) **evening** le soir *nm*
except sauf
exercise book le cahier *nm*
eyes les yeux *nm pl*

F

factory une usine *nf*
false faux/fausse *adj*
farm une ferme *nf*
father le père *nm*
fast-food restaurant *le fast food nm*
favourite préféré/préférée
February février
felt-tip pen le feutre *nm*
fifteen quinze
fifty cinquante
file un classeur *nm*
to **finish** finir *v*
first le premier *nm*/la première *nf*
on the **first floor** au premier étage
fish le poisson *nm*
fishing la pêche *nf*
five cinq
flag le drapeau *nm*
flat un appartement *nm*
floor *le plancher nm*
It is **foggy.** Il y a du brouillard.
football le foot(ball) *nm*
for pour
foreign étranger/étrangère *adj*
forty quarante
four quatre
fourteen quatorze
France la France *nf*
It is **freezing.** Il gèle.
French français/française *adj*
(on) Friday (le) vendredi
friend (male) un ami, un copain *nm*
friend (female) une amie, une copine *nf*
friends les amis, les copains *nm pl*
in **front of** devant
fun amusant/amusante *adj*
funny marrant/marrante *adj*

G

games console une console *nf*
garage *un garage nm*
garden le jardin *nm*
generally généralement; en général
generous généreux/généreuse *adj*
geography la géographie *nf*
German l'allemand *nm*
to **get dressed** s'habiller *v*
ginger(-haired) roux/rousse *adj*

girlfriend une petite amie *nf*
glass un verre *nm*
glue stick un bâton de colle *nm*
to **go** aller *v*
to **go to bed** se coucher *v*
goldfish un poisson rouge *nm*
golf le golf *nm*
goodbye au revoir; salut
gram un gramme *nm*
grandfather le grand-père *nm*
grandmother la grand-mère *nf*
grandparents les grands-parents *nm pl*
Great! Super! Génial!
green vert/verte *adj*
grey gris/grise *adj*
on the **ground floor** au rez-de-chaussée
guest house, bed and breakfast une chambre d'hôte *nf*
guinea pig le cochon d'Inde *nm*

H

hair les cheveux *nm pl*
half demi/demie *adj*
half-brother le demi-frère *nm*
half-sister la demi-sœur *nf*
ham le jambon *nm*
hamburger un hamburger *nm*
hamster un hamster *nm*
Happy birthday! Bon anniversaire!
harbour le port *nm*
hard difficile *adj*
hard-working travailleur/travailleuse *adj*
he/she/it **has** il/elle a
to **hate** détester *v*
to **have** avoir *v*
I **have** j'ai …
I don't **have** je n'ai pas …
they **have** ils/elles ont
we **have** (*informal*) on a
we **have** (*formal*) nous avons
you **have** (*informal*) tu as
you **have** (*formal*) vous avez
Have you got any pets (at home)? Tu as un animal (chez toi)?
he il
he is… il est…
Hello Bonjour
helmet un casque *nm*
her son/sa/ses
here is/here are … voici …
Here it is! Voilà!
Hi! Salut!
hiking la randonnée *nf*

his son/sa/ses
history l'histoire *nf*
hobbies les passe-temps *nm pl*
holiday camp une colonie de vacances nf
holiday cottage un gîte *nm*
to do **homework** faire *v* les devoirs
horse(s) le cheval (les chevaux) *nm*
to go **horse riding** faire *v* de l'équitation
hot chaud/chaude
It is **hot.** Il fait chaud.
hot chocolate le chocolat chaud *nm*
hour une heure *nf*
house la maison *nf*
How are you? Ça va?
How much? Combien?
How old are you? Tu as quel âge? *(to a friend or relative),* Vous avez quel âge? *(to more than one person, someone you don't know well)*

I

I je, j'
I am … je suis …
I am (11). J'ai (11) ans.
I can't wait j'ai très hâte
I come from… je viens de…
I don't have… je n'ai pas de…
I don't like… je n'aime pas…
I hate… je déteste…
I have… j'ai…
I like… j'aime…
I live in… (town) j'habite à…
I love… j'adore…
I'd like… je voudrais…
I'm fine. Ça va.
I'm sorry. Je suis désolé/désolée.
ice hockey le hockey sur glace *nm*
ice-skating le patinage *nm*
ice cream la glace *nf*
ICT l'informatique *nf*
in (France) en (France)
in (my bag) dans (mon sac)
in front of devant
in the country à la campagne
in the suburbs en banlieue
in town en ville
intelligent intelligent/intelligente *adj*
interesting intéressant/intéressante *adj*

Internet l'Internet *nm*
Ireland l'Irlande *nf*
Irish irlandais/irlandaise *adj*
Is there...? Il y a...?
it ça
It's... C'est...
It's a... C'est un/une...
It's (two) o'clock. Il est (deux) heures.
It's five past (two). Il est (deux) heures cinq.
It's five to (two). Il est (deux) heures moins cinq.
It's OK. Bof. Ça va.
It's spelt... Ça s'écrit...

jam la confiture *nf*
January janvier
July juillet
June juin

karaoke machine une machine à karaoké *nf*
kilo un kilo *nm*
kitchen la cuisine *nf*

lamp une lampe *nf*
last weekend le week-end dernier
lazy paresseux/ paresseuse *adj*
leg la jambe *nf*
lemon un citron *nm*
lemonade la limonade *nf*
lesson un cours *nm*
less than moins que
library la bibliothèque *nf*
I **like...** J'aime...
I don't **like...** Je n'aime pas...
to **listen to music** écouter *v* de la musique
to **live** habiter
living room le salon *nm*
long long/longue *adj*
to **look after children** garder *v* des enfants
to **look at** regarder *v*
lots of beaucoup de
I **love...** J'adore...
lunch le déjeuner *nm*

Madam Madame
to **make** faire *v*
to **make my bed** faire *v* mon lit
March mars
maths les maths *nf pl*
May mai
meal un plat *nm*
Me too. Moi aussi.
to **meet friends** retrouver *v* des amis
memory stick une clé USB *nf*
midday midi
midnight minuit
milk le lait *nm*
milk shake un milk-shake *nm*
mineral water l'eau minérale *nf*
mirror un miroir *nm*
Miss Mademoiselle
to **mix** mélanger *v*
(on) **Monday** (le) lundi
more than plus que
morning le matin *nm*
mother la mère *nf*
mountaineering l'alpinisme *nm*
mouse la souris *nf*
Mr Monsieur
MP3 player/walkman un baladeur (MP3) *nm*
Mrs Madame
museum le musée *nm*
music la musique *nf*
music programme une émission musicale *nf*
my mon/ma/mes
My birthday's on... Mon anniversaire, c'est le...
at **my house** chez moi
My name is... Je m'appelle...

name le nom *nm*
the **news** les informations *nf pl*
nice sympa *adj*
nine neuf
nineteen dix-neuf
ninety quatre-vingt-dix
no non
no, thank you non, merci
north le nord *nm*
not me pas moi
November novembre

October octobre
of de
OK d'accord
on sur
one un/une
one hundred cent
only child (female) fille unique *nf*
only child (male) fils unique *nm*
opinion l'opinion *nf*
or ou
orange (fruit) une orange *nf*
orange (colour) orange *adj*
orange juice un jus d'orange *nm*

packet un paquet *nm*
pancake une crêpe *nf*
pancake restaurant une crêperie *nf*
parents les parents *nm pl*
park le parc *nm*
pâté le pâté *nm*
patient patient/patiente *adj*
PE l'EPS *nm*; le sport *nm*
peas les petits pois *nm pl*
pen un stylo *nm*
pencil un crayon *nm*
pencil case une trousse *nf*
pencil sharpener un taille-crayon *nm*
pepper le poivre *nm*
petrol l'essence *nf*
physics la physique *nf*
pineapple l'ananas *nm*
pink rose *adj*
pizza la pizza *nf*
pizzeria la pizzeria *nf*
plane l'avion *nm*
platform le quai *nm*
player le/la joueur/joueuse *nm/f*
to **play sport** faire *v* du sport
please s'il te plaît *(to a friend or relative)*, s'il vous plaît *(to more than one person, someone you don't know well)*
posh snob
TV programme une émission

Q

It's **quarter past (two).** Il est (deux) heures et quart.
It's **quarter to (three).** Il est (trois) heures moins le quart.
quiet calme *adj*
quite assez

R

rabbit un lapin *nm*
railway station la gare SNCF *nf*
It's **raining.** Il pleut.
RE la religion *nf*
reading la lecture *nf*
reality TV programme une émission de télé realité *nf*
really vraiment
red rouge *adj*
to go **rock climbing** faire de l'escalade
rubber une gomme *nf*
rubbish les ordures *nf pl*
rug le tapis *nm*
rugby le rugby *nm*
ruler une règle *nf*

S

to go **sailing** faire *v* de la voile
salt le sel *nm*
sandwich un sandwich *nm*
(on) **Saturday** (le) samedi
high **school** le collège *nm*
science les sciences *nf pl*
scissors les ciseaux *nm pl*
Scotland l'Écosse *nf*
seafood les fruits de mer *nm pl*
on the **second floor** au deuxième étage
the **second (of May)** le deux (mai)
See you soon. À bientôt.
see you later à tout à l'heure
selfish égoïste *adj*
sensible sérieux/sérieuse *adj*
September septembre
series une série *nf*
to **set the table** mettre le couvert *v*
seven sept
seventeen dix-sept
seventy soixante-dix
she elle
she is... elle est...
shelf une étagère *nf*
short (hair) (les cheveux) courts *adj*
shy timide *adj*
Sir Monsieur

sister une sœur *nf*
sitting room le salon *nm*
six six
sixteen seize
sixty soixante
to go **skateboarding** faire *v* du skate
slice une tranche *nf*
slim mince *adj*
small petit/petite *adj*
snake un serpent *nm*
It's **snowing.** Il neige.
soap opera un feuilleton *nm*
some des
sometimes quelquefois
soup la soupe *nf*
south le sud *nm*
Spanish l'espagnol *nm*
spectator le/la spectateur/spectatrice *nm/f*
It's **spelt...** Ça s'écrit...
to do **sport** faire *v* du sport
sports centre le centre sportif *nm*
sports programme une émission sportive *nf*
sporty sportif/sportive *adj*
spots les boutons *nm pl*
spring le printemps *nm*
to **start** commencer *v*
(railway) **station** la gare *nf*
to **stay** loger *v*
step-brother le demi-frère *nm*
step-father le beau-père *nm*
step-mother la belle-mère *nf*
step-sister la demi-sœur *nf*
It's **stormy.** Il y a de l'orage.
straight (hair) (les cheveux) raides *adj*
stubborn têtu/têtue *adj*
suburbs la banlieue *nf*
sugar le sucre *nm*
summer l'été *nm*
sun le soleil *nm*
(on) **Sunday** (le) dimanche
It's **sunny.** Il y a du soleil.
super super
supermarket le supermarché *nm*
to go **surfing** faire *v* du surf
to go **swimming** faire *v* de la natation *nf*
swimming pool la piscine *nf*

T

table tennis le ping-pong *nm*
to **take** prendre *v*
tall grand/grande *adj*
tea (with milk) le thé (au lait)

nm
teacher le professeur *nm*
technology la technologie *nf*
teeth les dents *nf pl*
ten dix
tennis le tennis *nm*
terrible affreux/affreuse *adj*
It's **terrible.** C'est nul.
thank you merci
the le/la/les
there are... il y a...
there aren't any... il n'y a pas de...
there is... il y a...
there isn't any... il n'y a pas de...
they ils/elles
on the **third floor** au troisième étage
on the **third (of May)** le trois (mai)
thirteen treize
thirty trente
three trois
(on) **Thursday** (le) jeudi
ticket un billet *nm*
to **tidy** ranger *v*
tin une boîte *nf*
tiring fatigant/fatigante *adj*
to à
today aujourd'hui
toilet les toilettes *nf pl*
tomato une tomate *nf*
tortoise une tortue *nf*
tourist office l'office du tourisme *nm*
town la ville *nf*
town centre le centre-ville *nm*
traffic la circulation *nf*
train le train *nm*
true vrai/vraie *adj*
(on) **Tuesday** (le) mardi
tuna le thon *nm*
TV la télé(vision) *nf*
TV game show un jeu télévisé *nm*
twelve douze
twenty vingt
twenty-one vingt et un
two deux

U

uncle un oncle *nm*
under sous
USB stick une clé USB *nf*

very très
village un village *nm*
volleyball le volley-ball *nm*

Wales le pays de Galles *nm*
wardrobe une armoire *nf*
war film un film de guerre
to **wash** se laver *v*
to **watch (TV)** regarder *v* (la télé)
water l'eau *nf*
water-skiing le ski nautique *nm*
we on *(informal)*,
 nous *(formal)*
weather le temps *nm*
website *un site web nm*
(on) **Wednesday** (le) mercredi
week la semaine *nf*
well bien
well-built gros/grosse *adj*
Welsh *gallois/galloise adj*
west l'ouest *nm*
western un western *nm*
What...? Qu'est-ce que...?
What about you? Et toi?
What is... like? Comment
 est...?
What is there...? Qu'est-ce
 qu'il y a...?
What's your name? Tu t'appelles
 comment?
When? Quand?
Where? Où?
Where are...? Où sont...?
Where do you live? Tu habites
 où?
Where is...? Où est...?
Which...? Quel...?/Quelle...?
white blanc/blanche *adj*
whiteboard *un tableau blanc nm*
Who? Qui?
Why? Pourquoi?
window une fenêtre *nf*
to go **windsurfing** faire *v* de la
 planche à voile
It's **windy** Il y a du vent.
winter l'hiver *nm*
worse pire *adv*
the **worst** le/la pire *m/f*
I **would like...** Je voudrais...

yellow jaune *adj*
yes oui
yesterday hier
you tu *(to a friend or
 relative)*, vous *(to more than
 one person, someone you don't
 know well)*
you are... tu es..., vous êtes...
your ton/ta/tes, votre/vos
at **your house** chez toi
youth club le club des jeunes *nm*
youth hostel une auberge de
 jeunesse (AJ) *nf*